Gardens of the Arts and Crafts Movement

Troughery garden at Rodmarton Manor, Gloucestershire, 1993

Gardens of the Arts and Crafts Movement

Reality and Imagination

By Judith B. Tankard

Harry N. Abrams, Inc., Publishers

Contents

Preface. In recent years, the Arts and Crafts Movement has been enthusiastically hailed by historians, architects, designers, antique dealers, and a host of entrepreneurs. Its rich legacy of architecture and decorative objects continues to inspire designers and homeowners alike. Museums on both sides of the Atlantic boast collections of the work of the movement's star designers and surviving houses, furniture, textiles, wallpapers, ceramics, metalwork, and books gloriously portray this short-lived, but enlightened period of design that was cut short by World War I. A romance continues to be spun about this magical era and its icons, such as William Morris's Red House in England and the Gamble House in America. What is sometimes overlooked is the fact that the movement was a philosophical approach to design, rather than an identifiable style.

While much has been written about the architecture and decorative arts of the period, its landscape design has rarely been discussed. Few gardens designed over one hundred years ago survive in any recognizable form today, and gardens are often seen as isolated entities, dismissed as the sum of their plantings rather than properly understood for their function in an overall scheme. The Arts and Crafts Movement gave gardens new definition as a harmonious component of the house. It is, in fact, impossible to appreciate garden design of the Arts and Crafts era without understanding the house, nor the house without its garden.

This book takes as its theme the inspiration, characteristics, and development of garden design during the Arts and Crafts era. Not surprisingly, William Morris, who stands at the heart of the Arts and Crafts Movement, provided the fundamental philosophy for these gardens. The Arts and Crafts Movement, which was concerned with raising the standards of architecture and design, owes its greatest debt to Morris. In his own homes and his writings, he demonstrated how gardens were as integral to the home as its architecture and furnishings. Morris's followers provided individualistic and regional stamps to the basic tenets of Morris's philosophy.

Arts and Crafts gardens are not nearly as complex and self-conscious as such iconic modern gardens as Hidcote and Sissinghurst, which are composed of distinct garden rooms that may or may not relate to the dwelling house. Arts and Crafts gardens were conceived on a more intimate scale, with well-crafted detailing and a special approach to planting design. They were never an end in themselves, but were intertwined with the house like ivy growing on a wall, blurring the distinctions between indoors and outdoors. Their simple structuring and romantic, medieval-inspired imagery derived from old English manor house gardens. Nothing about them was ostentatious, contrived, or "foreign." Handbuilt stone walls, summerhouses, sundials, and other traditional ornament, hedged enclosures, colorful flower borders, and whimsical topiaried trees made for memorable storybook gardens.

This book presents a highly personal selection of houses and gardens of the Arts and Crafts era, with an emphasis on the diversity of designers who helped forge a special approach to garden design. For every house and garden that was built, there were many equally innovative, but unrealized schemes that went no further than the drawing board. In this book, Arts and Crafts gardens are presented through the eyes of artists and the words of designers and critics, drawing on the most influential publications of the era: *Country Life* magazine, *The Studio* magazine, *Gardens for Small Country Houses,* and *The Art and Craft of Garden-Making.* The thread of Gertrude Jekyll runs through most of the chapters of this book due to her collaboration with many Arts and Crafts architects, her finely honed planting skills, and incomparable writings.

While the Arts and Crafts Movement eventually fell into disfavor due to changing aesthetics and altered economic conditions, it left a rich legacy throughout Britain, where its influence was felt in the Garden City Movement and later filtered down to ordinary suburban homes. It left an unmistakable imprint on American architecture and gardens through the 1920s. In America, its influence touched on amateur gardeners who responded with a homespun Craftsman style, as well as on architects, designers, and reformers who tempered the movement's fundamental ideology to the country's diverse regionalism. More recently, a renewed interest in traditional building crafts and small, formal gardens returns the movement to the forefront.

While a graduate student in art history in the 1960s, I was first introduced to the world of Arts and Crafts architects and designers, notably William Morris and C.F.A. Voysey, whose wallpaper designs were the subject of my master's thesis. Having grown up in a house permeated with American Victorian furnishings avidly collected by my parents, I found that the Arts and Crafts era offered a breath of fresh air. Living then in Forest Hills Gardens, an ideal garden suburb designed by Frederick Law Olmsted, Jr., and Grosvenor Atterbury, may have sparked a slumbering awareness of landscape architecture and English-inspired domestic architecture. A seminal visit to Standen in 1965, while it was still owned by the original family, opened my eyes to another world. Helen Beale welcomed us with homemade scones dripping with butter and cream that had gone sour in the dairy and regaled us with her youthful memories of the dashing Philip Webb, heavily enveloped in a large cape, arriving on the building site. Years later, my discovery of Edwin Lutyens and Gertrude Jekyll cemented my addiction to the Arts and Crafts Movement and unwittingly thrust me into the relatively new discipline of garden design history.

My book has grown from a desire to present Arts and Crafts gardens in the broad context of art, architecture, interior design, and decorative arts in which they need to be appreciated. It was fueled by my personal library of period books and magazines devoted to architecture, garden design, and decorative arts as well as a personal collection of paintings and decorative arts by artists and designers of the era. This approach definitely has its limitations and I leave it to others to write the penultimate studies on American Arts and Crafts gardens and the ramifications of the movement on international garden design.

JUDITH B. TANKARD, NOVEMBER 2003

Introduction. In the 1870s England began to emerge from the heavy shroud of Victorian design sensibilities by embracing a new aesthetic that would have ramifications on the design of houses, interiors, and decorative arts until the First World War. The Aesthetic Movement, which centered around the world of James McNeill Whistler and Oscar Wilde, ushered in a new concept in domestic architecture and interior design known as the "The House Beautiful."[1] The concept of artistic houses characterized by the lightness of their interiors and decorated with beautiful objects, was a welcome relief from the heavy furnishings, dark interiors, and somber palette of the Victorian era. This new aesthetic was especially appealing to the growing middle classes with new-found artistic yearnings.

The parallel Queen Anne Movement, with its distinctive style of architecture that harkened back to an earlier period in English history, took hold in London's newly fashionable enclaves, such as Chelsea and Bedford Park. The leading architect was Richard Norman Shaw (1831–1912) who, along with Ernest J. May, designed the artists' suburb in Bedford Park. There, red brick houses had picturesque turrets and gables, and artistic interiors in soft, pleasing colors. The Queen Anne style was personified in nursery books written and illustrated by Walter Crane, Randolph Caldecott, and, above all, Kate Greenaway, whose *Under the Window* (1878), *Mother Goose* (1881), *A Day in a Child's Life* (1881), and *Marigold Garden* (1885) depict caricatures of Shaw houses. Her own brick house in Hampstead was designed by Shaw in 1885. Children decked out in sunbonnets play outdoors amidst green croquet lawns and gardens filled with colorful flower borders and enormous topiaried shrubs and trees. The steep-roofed red tile roofs of houses peek over the tops of high green hedges and

Kate Greenaway (1846–1900). *Afternoon Tea* (from *The Girl's Own Paper*

Ernest Newton, Fouracre, West Green, Hampshire, watercolor by T. Hamilton Crawford, 1902. RIBA Library Drawings Collection, London
Below: Philip Webb, Standen, East Grinstead, West Sussex, 1992

afternoon tea on the lawn with flower borders bursting with sunflowers and roses and the Shaw-inspired house on the other side of the wall.

The Queen Anne style, for all its quaintness, was more suited to townhouses, shops, and suburban areas than to country houses, for which something more traditionally "English" was called for.[2] It was during this period that former country seats were replaced by smaller houses inspired by old English models of many forms. According to Ernest Newton (1856–1922), one of Shaw's pupils, these pioneer architects "aimed at catching the spirit of the old building rather than at the literal reproduction of any defined style."[3] Newton's genteel houses, such as Fouracre, in West Green, Hampshire, of 1901, defi-

Thomas H. Hunn, (1857–1928), *Great Tangley Manor, Surrey,* watercolor, c. 1900. Christopher Wood Gallery, London

nitely catch this spirit. The red-brick house with decorative bands of trim, and the front door opening out onto the garden, is simple, genial, and welcoming. As with many of the architects of the era, Newton's career advanced from Queen Anne and Tudor to Georgian revivals.

Shaw was a versatile architect best known for his old English style; his country houses were generously sized, with half-timbering and other traditional details. In addition to Shaw, the leading practitioners of the new architecture were George Devey and Philip Webb. George Devey (1820–1886), a superb watercolor artist known for his picturesque approach to design, was one of the first Victorian architects to create houses based on the local vernacular, an important issue for Arts and Crafts architects.[4]

Devey's sympathetic restorations of older buildings were drawn from an extensive knowledge of Elizabethan and Jacobean architecture.

Philip Speakman Webb (1831–1915) undoubtedly had the most far-reaching influence of the trio. His houses evoke the old in detailing, but are innovative in planning, reflecting his passion for traditional building and local materials without copying them in a historicist fashion. A master of understatement, Webb profoundly influenced the coming generation of architects. Standen, designed in 1891 for the London solicitor James Beale, is his masterpiece. The brick and stone house, with its distinctive wooden gables and tile-hung facade, takes its cue from the old farm buildings on the site that other architects might have torn down. Webb's unusual sensitivity to vernacular buildings and details had an enormous influence on the design of country houses in England.

At Great Tangley Manor, near Guildford in Surrey, Webb redesigned and extended a half-timbered house, with origins in the sixteenth century, in 1886. He returned in 1894 to add a stone library wing that complemented the old half-timbered front. Webb's garden architecture included a timber-roofed bridge over the moat and a rustic pergola. These improvements drew considerable comment from Gertrude Jekyll, who lived nearby and had known the house in its former, more dilapidated and overgrown state. The ancient enclosure, with its arched doorway and loop-holed walls, inspired Edwin Lutyens at Millmead and elsewhere.[5] The flower borders within the enclosure, which were so characteristic of the era, were filled with a pleasurable mixture of lilies, irises, larkspurs, and other hardy perennials.

Small country houses within easy reach of London for weekend retreats for the upper middle class would become the realm of a new generation of architects, mostly born in the 1860s, who trained in some of the most prestigious offices of the day. In addition to Newton and May, Shaw's office produced William R. Lethaby (a major theorist of the era), Gerald Horsley, Mervyn Macartney (the influential editor of *The Architectural Review*), Edward S. Prior, and Robert Weir Schultz. Ernest George's office trained Herbert Baker, Guy Dawber, and Edwin Lutyens, while John Sedding's office trained both Ernest Barnsley and Ernest Gimson.[6] Beginning in the 1890s, these architects, and a host of others, would create some of the signature examples of domestic architecture associated with the Arts and Crafts Movement, bringing England to the forefront of architectural design.

Unquestionably the stars were Edwin Lutyens, whose romantic Surrey houses built from local stone gave new definition to the concept of vernacular; C.F.A. Voysey, whose quirky, white-washed roughcast houses and quaint garden furnishings were universally hailed; and M. H. Baillie Scott, whose half-timbered suburban cottages had a profound impact on domestic architecture. Despite the various sources of design inspiration, whether Gothic Revival, Byzantine Revival, Classicism, or Vernacular, all these architects were united by their staunch individualism, regionalism, and respect for building arts.

In the early 1900s it took an enlightened foreigner to appreciate the importance of architectural developments in England. Hermann Muthesius (1861–1927), the court-appointed

Thomas H. Hunn (1857–1928), *The Lily Border at Great Tangley Manor, Surrey*, watercolor, c. 1900. Christopher Wood Gallery, London

attaché to the German Embassy in London, extolled the new "free" style in his three-volume work, *Das Englische Haus*, the result of his detailed study of English domestic architecture. While living in Hammersmith, he fell in with the Morris circle and came to admire the recent work of Shaw, Lethaby, Voysey, and Charles Rennie Mackintosh. Muthesius credited the phenomenon of the English country house to the Englishman's desire for "sincerity and unpretentiousness" in his house, as well as the avoidance of any kind of display, rather than deliberately aiming at a specifically modern look. "The fundamental traits of the English house are its reserve, modesty, and charming sincerity."[7] He singled out Gertrude Jekyll's Munstead Wood as a worthy contrast to the English house of fifty years earlier, a period he considered a low point in domestic architecture.

Sparked by John Ruskin, William Morris, and their followers who called for design reform based on simplicity and utility, the new movement championed the England of happier, pre-industrial days. Picture books and paintings of the latter part of the nineteenth century portrayed a romanticized rural England, its landscapes, vernacular architecture, traditional crafts, and leisurely pursuits. The artist Helen Allingham's book *Happy England* (1903) paints an evocative picture of the English countryside filled with quaint cottages, lush flower borders, and beautiful children. Allingham's nostalgic view of country life is one seemingly devoid of hardships and the negative effects of industrialization.[8] Legions of artists, poets, and writers extolled the virtues of country living as opposed to the grim realities of city life. The back-to-the-land movement was sparked by a new-found reverence for the unspoiled English countryside and its rural traditions as an escape from the unhealthful atmosphere of cities, as well as their inherent social strictures. Ruskin's plea for deeper moral values, including recognition of artists and artisans alike, was only one manifestation of the underlying social dissatisfaction of the day.

The Arts and Crafts Movement emerged from deep moral and social concerns. The complexity of the movement's origins, ideals, and manifestations has been the subject of many detailed studies, but its basic tenets were a fundamental disdain for the falseness of High Victorian design, a rediscovery of nature and English traditions, and the idea that manual work could be personally fulfilling.[9] Inspired by Morris, the movement sought to bring together architects and craftsmen to work in harmony. The founding of the Art Workers' Guild in 1884 by a group of Shaw's assistants for the purpose of providing a meeting place for architects and craftworkers to discuss their work quickly fused together some of the movement's early objectives.[10] One of the guild's early ventures was the establishment of the Arts and Crafts Exhibition Society, which eventually provided a name to the new movement. Beginning with its first exhibition of members' work in 1888, it served to spread the word about design reform. Beginning in 1893, *The Studio* magazine published illustrations of their architectural perspectives, garden designs, metalwork and jewelry, ceramics, textiles, and wallpapers, all of which rubbed shoulders happily with one another.

The Arts and Crafts Movement championed the unity of the arts, in which the house, the furnishing of its interiors, and the garden were considered a whole, or as Muthesius expressed it, "garden, house, and interior—a unity."[11] The parallel revival of the art of garden design came into play at a time when architects not only saw to every detail of the house and its interiors, but routinely laid out the gardens. These gardens, with their neatly clipped hedges and ordered geometry, harkened back to the England of the sixteenth and seventeenth centuries, the pleasure grounds of the Tudors and Stuarts. In contrast to nineteenth-century estate gardens that were vast in scale and stiffly planted with brightly colored annuals and jarring foliage, gardens designed by Arts and Crafts architects and their collaborators were intimate in scale, with soothing colors and textures. They harmonized perfectly with the house and were often distinguished by individualistic architectural components, such as garden houses, dovecotes, and pergolas, all constructed in the local materials of the region.

Helen Allingham (1848–1926), *Cottage Near Brook, Witley, Surrey*, watercolor. Christopher Wood Gallery, London

Chapter 1 | Gardens Old and New. Changing attitudes about garden design in late-nineteenth-century England reflected the undercurrents of unrest in architecture and design. John Sedding, Reginald Blomfield, H. Inigo Triggs, and other architect-theorists began to re-evaluate gardens and their ideal configuration. They rejected both the horticulturally driven gardens of the Victorian era and the idealized nature of the eighteenth-century landscape style.[1] What emerged during this period were theoretical debates representing two different viewpoints, pitting the architects against the horticulturists.

Blomfield's highly influential book, *The Formal Garden in England*, first published in 1892 and still considered a key work of the period, was the first to adopt the word "formal" to describe the architectural gardens of the Tudor and Renaissance periods that he proposed as models for "new" gardens. Blomfield had little interest in horticulture. As he wrote, "Horticulture stands to garden design much as building does to architecture; the two are connected, but very far from being identical."[2] Even Hermann Muthesius, who distanced himself somewhat from these debates, remarked that in England it was typical for the design of the garden to be placed in the hands of the architect, whose role was to conceive it in relationship to the house, while the gardener was left to execute it.[3] According to Ernest Newton, architects who in the past had been forced to delegate the laying out of garden to "alien hands" rejoiced at the "dethronement of the nursery gardener [who specialized in] the cult of the curly path, of the kidney-shaped bed and clump of pampas grass."[4] This stance, which was shared by other architects of the era, was held in disdain by horticulturists and gardeners alike, who countered that architects knew nothing about garden design.

Blomfield singled out George Devey for his successful efforts in designing house and grounds in relation to one another. In the 1840s, Devey had revitalized the ancient gardens at Penshurst Place in Kent for Lord de L'Isle when he restored the old house with origins dating to the sixteenth century. His sensitive refurbishment of the gardens set the precedent for future generations of architects to draw upon. Some of the individual compartments were surrounded

Ernest Arthur Rowe (1863–1922), *Penshurst Place, Kent,* watercolor, 1895. Christopher Wood Gallery, London

by yew hedges or walls within the original asymmetrical configuration. The grander formal gardens, on axis with the house, include two ornamental orchard gardens and a large parterre. The central pool and fountain set within a patterned framework of low hedges are depicted in Ernest Arthur Rowe's watercolor of 1891. A dense backdrop of ancient trees among the old buildings was the perfect setting for the garden.

Reginald Blomfield's career owed much to the success of his book on garden design. An early supporter of the Arts and Crafts Movement, Blomfield (1856–1942) was a member of the Art Workers' Guild and a partner in Kenton and Company, a short-lived business enterprise specializing in handmade furniture that was a predecessor to some of the regional craft guilds that sprang up later.[5] In the course of his work, which was mostly devoted to the classical style, he was frequently asked to design gardens evoking the old English style.

Godinton House in Kent, with its smooth lawns, terraces, distinctive topiary, and hedges clipped to reflect the gables of the house, serves as a good example of his elementary garden-planning skills. One of his best-known commissions is the large formal garden at Mellerstain House in the Scottish Borders, an exceptionally fine Georgian house built by William Adam in 1725, with later additions by his famous son, Robert Adam. Blomfield's garden, laid out in 1909 and consisting of twin parterres, with terraces overlooking the Cheviot Hills, unfortunately obliterated the earlier canal garden that was more appropriate to the period of the house. Although a successful architect, Blomfield's historical interpretation of gardens was often fanciful.

Another early-twentieth-century book that extolled the architectural gardens of the sixteenth and seventeenth centuries as models for "new" gardens is *Formal Gardens in*

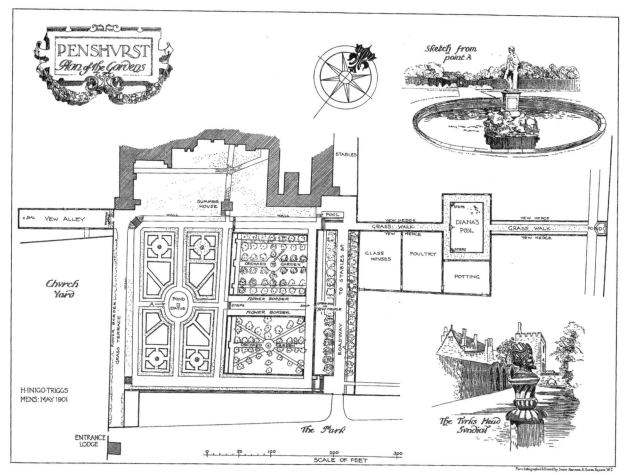

H. Inigo Triggs, *Penshurst: Plan of the Gardens*, line drawing, 1901 (from Triggs, *Formal Gardens in England and Scotland*, 1902, plate 14). Author's Collection

Overleaf: *Montacute House, Somerset*, 1990

England and Scotland (1902), a lavish folio measuring 13" x 17" with exquisitely drawn plans and elevations of historic gardens. It was prepared by Harry Inigo Triggs (1876–1923), a young architect who specialized in romantic Elizabethan houses and sunken water gardens. *Gardens Old and New* (1901–07), a three-volume compendium of articles first published in *Country Life* and illustrated with sumptuous photographs, glorified the best of England's *old* historic gardens as well as *new* gardens designed along old themes.

Ironically, by the end of the nineteenth century, little survived of most manor house gardens of the sixteenth and early seventeenth centuries, except possibly the original outlines. Montacute House, in Somerset, which was hailed in many period books, including Blomfield's and Triggs's, took most of its identity from a restoration of the early 1890s. Montacute's simple garden layout, as rendered by Triggs, is basically a

series of formal garden terraces. The Upper Garden is a simple bowling green or lawn with ancient cedar trees, and the North Garden is broken into four quadrants with a central pool and fountain. The central courtyard, with the distinctive detailing of its walls and its twin garden pavilions, served as an inspiration for architects who were actively engaged in restoring old gardens as well as creating new ones that evoked the old. Gertrude Jekyll wryly noted, however, that the obelisk-shaped finials at Montacute "were borrowed straight from the Italians [but without] their marvelous discernment."[6]

Francis Inigo Thomas (1866–1950), Blomfield's protégé who prepared the drawings for *The Formal Garden in England*, excelled at restoring and remodeling existing gardens, using the vocabulary of older gardens.[7] At Athelhampton, a late-fifteenth-century manor house in Dorset, he rehabilitated the deteriorating old hall and made a new garden in the old man-

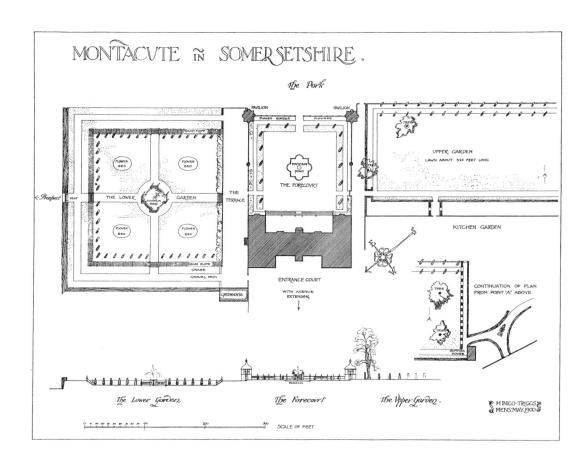

Above:

H. Inigo Triggs, Montacute in
Somerset, line drawing, 1900
(from Triggs, Formal Gardens in
England and Scotland, 1902,
plate 1). Author's Collection

Opposite top:

H. Inigo Triggs, Montacute
House: The Garden House and
Pavilion, line drawing, 1900
(from Triggs, Formal Gardens in
England and Scotland, 1902,
plate 2). Author's Collection

Opposite middle:

Simon Dorrell, Athelhampton,
ink drawing (Hortus, Winter
1984)

Opposite bottom:
Parnham, Dorset, 1990

ner by creating a series of interrelating enclosures evoking
those of the Elizabethan era, with specific quotations from
Montacute. The enclosure walls were built from warm-colored
Ham stone, acquired not far from Montacute in Somerset.[8] At
the center of the garden, he added a circular Coronet (or
Corona), with raised stone obelisks on the surrounding wall
and a circular pool, and adjacent to this is a large rectangular
garden, or Great Court, with two garden houses. This garden is
distinguished by dramatic rows of pyramidal yews, with a central basin and fountain. On axis with the house, and on the
other side of the Coronet, lies the third enclosure, a companion
pool garden. In all, it was the quintessence of an architectural
garden. Parnham, also in Dorset, and thought to have been
designed by Thomas, also has many echoes of Montacute,
including its balustrading, obelisks, and two pavilions.

Gothic Revival architect John Dando Sedding (1838–1891),
who had an affinity for decorations drawn from nature, wrote
another important treatise on garden design, *Garden-Craft
Old and New* (1890), in which he presented a practical, if

romanticized, approach to the design of gardens. It laid the foundation for Arts and Crafts gardens in the early 1900s. "The old-fashioned garden," Sedding wrote, "represents one of the pleasures of England, one of the charms of that quiet beautiful life of bygone times." Because these gardens are "beautiful yesterday, beautiful to-day, and beautiful always. . . we do well to turn to them, not to copy their exact lines, nor to limit ourselves to the range of their ornament and effects, but to glean hints for our garden-enterprise to-day, to drink of their spirit, to gain impulsion from them."[9] Sedding championed the "garden enclosed," with high box hedges and ornamented with flower borders and whimsical yew topiaries clipped into bird-like forms that were beloved of the Arts and Crafts architects.

Old-fashioned gardens, with their smooth bowling greens, massive hedges, overflowing flower borders, clipped topiaries, and other characteristic vocabulary, formed the basis for new gardens made by architects during the Arts and Crafts era.

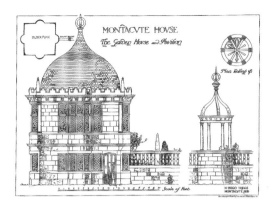

Walter Crane's pictorial cover for *A Floral Fantasy in an Old English Garden* captures the essence of an old-fashioned garden, with its hedged enclosure, spade-shaped tubbed trees of improbable height, and topiaried peacocks.[10] A sundial and simple garden gate complete the scene.

Billowing hedges and fanciful clipped **topiaries** were emblematic of old English gardens. Topiary took many inventive forms, from cakestands and spirals to hatted heads and chessmen, each identified with a specific garden, such as Levens Hall and Montacute. The historic topiary gardens at Levens Hall, in Cumbria, which date to the late seventeenth century, are probably the most outstanding example of their kind. "Near the house," according to a description in 1884, "are pyramids with balls at top and bastionettes fashioned in their angles, arbours impenetrable to sun or rain or peering eyes, tall mushrooms on slender stalks, and other quaint devices."[11]

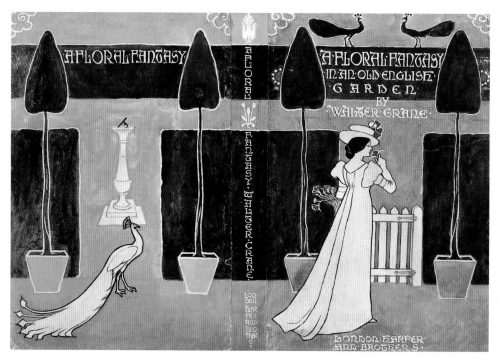

Walter Crane (1845–1915), *A Floral Fantasy in an Old English Garden,* watercolor design for book jacket, 1899. Victoria and Albert Museum, London

Plate 106

25

GARDENS OLD AND NEW

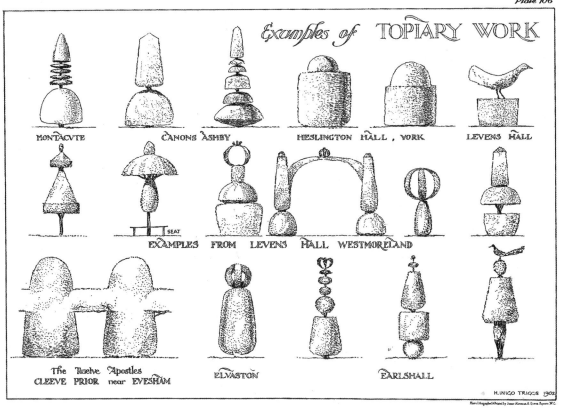

H. Inigo Triggs, Examples of Topiary Work, line drawing, 1902 (from Triggs, *Formal Gardens in England and Scotland,* 1902, plate 106). Author's Collection

In 1905 Jekyll praised the gardens at Levens as a perfect complement to the house, "growing with it into a complete harmony of mellow age."[12]

Brickwall, in Northiam, East Sussex, is an equally remarkable green garden, with origins dating to 1680, when it was laid out by the Frewen family. In 1873, Devey remodeled the timber-framed Jacobean house, adding a new front with half-timbered gables overlooking the garden.[13] Nearly thirty years after Devey's addition had been allowed to mellow, Jekyll commented that Brickwall was a "delightful example, both as to house and garden, of these old places of the truest English type. . . . the garden [being] laid out to view, almost as a picture hangs on a wall, in the very best position for the convenience of the spectator."[14] The garden consists of two major sections, separated by double flower borders filled with plants that Jane Frewen might have selected in the late seventeenth century. A long line of pyramidal clipped yews frame the view

to the house from the nearer compartment, which once had a long reflecting pool. Jekyll praised the simplicity of the clipped yews, observing that they are best kept to one form or shape rather than a medley of forms, as found in other places.

A necessary adjunct to topiary gardens is a wide bowling green lined with clipped hedges, and beyond a tree-shaded walk and perhaps wild parkland. At Berkeley Castle, a twelfth-century battlemented castle not far from the Severn River in Gloucestershire, a long bowling green is banked by ancient yew hedges on three sides. "The yews, still clipped into bold rounded forms, may have formed a trim hedge in Tudor days, and the level space of turf . . . lies cool and sheltered from the westering sun by the stout bulwark of their ancient shade," wrote Jekyll who was a frequent visitor to the castle.[15] Dense flower borders, filled with hardy English plants, form a foil for the dark green hedges and the smooth lawn.

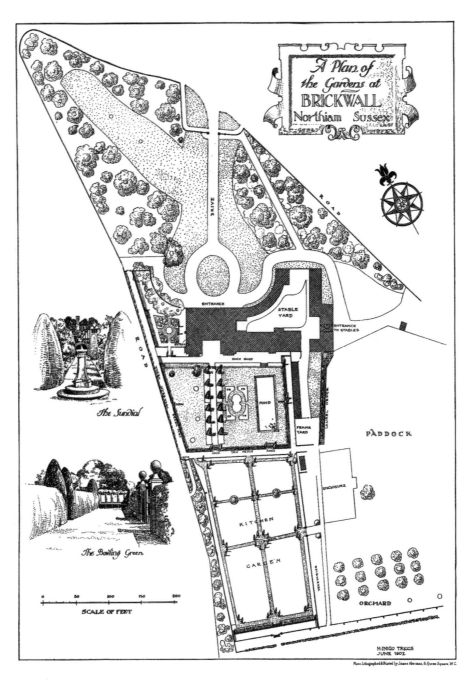

Above:
H. Inigo Triggs, The Plan of the
Gardens at Brickwall, line draw-
ing, 1902 (from Triggs, *Formal
Gardens in England and Scotland,*
1902, plate 50). Author's
Collection

Opposite top:
Gardens at Brickwall, East Sussex,
1986

Opposite bottom:
*Topiary garden at Levens Hall,
Cumbria,* 1987

Sedding's and Blomfield's books left no question in Muthesius's mind that the geometric garden should replace the landscape garden. "It is inconceivable that anyone in England today with a genuine concern for art could question its rightness," he asserted.[16] But these books drew the wrath of William Robinson, the era's most vocal horticulturist and promoter of the gardenesque approach to garden design. In *Garden Design and Architects' Gardens* (1892), Robinson took both books and their authors to task. His subtitle, "Two reviews, illustrated, to show, by actual examples from British gardens, that clipping and aligning trees to make them 'harmonise' with architecture is barbarous, needless, and inartistic," passionately expressed his heart-felt disdain for architects' gardens. Both books, he claimed, were "made up in great part of quotations from old books on gardening—many written by men who knew books better than gardening." In short, they contributed nothing to the "beautiful art of gardening or garden design."[17] He singled out Sedding's book as one devoted to "vegetable sculpture [written by someone] without any knowledge of plants, trees, or landscape beauty."[18]

Beyond the heat of the moment—and the controversy simmered for many years—was the reasonable viewpoint that hardy plants in naturalistic settings were the foundation of any garden. Robinson, who was known as the "Father of the English Flower Garden," took up the cause for Englishness in garden design and in choice of plants in the 1870s, long before the voices of either Blomfield or Sedding were heard. Robinson championed the same native English plants that William Morris used in his wallpapers and textiles. Robinson's numerous books favoring naturalistic groupings of hardy perennials were far more popular among gardeners than Sedding's or Blomfield's books.

While informal flower borders and naturalistic sweeps on woodland plants were important considerations, most of the gardens associated with the Arts and Crafts Movement were architectural, rather than horticultural, in concept. These gardens owe their greatest debt to traditional ones as extolled by Sedding and his followers. Their compartmentalized spaces and structural framework based on enclosing hedges or walls served as prototypes for small country house gardens designed by a younger generation of imaginative archi-

tects, some of whom had been pupils in Sedding's office. They opted for "old-time" accessories, such as sundials and armillary spheres, rather than classically inspired fountains and the stiff formality typically found in Victorian gardens.

Arts and Crafts gardens, which are distinguished by their exceptional architectural detailing, exemplary craftsmanship, emerald-green lawns, simple flower borders, and neatly clipped hedges, provided inviting, yet secluded outdoor spaces adjacent to the house. In their purist form, these gardens were designed by architects, some of whom had little knowledge of horticulture, rather than by horticulturists. Every architect, according to Muthesius, "considers it his duty to design the garden in conjunction with the house and to steep himself in the principles of garden design as in those of the art of furnishing a room."[19]

Beatrice Parsons (1870–1955), *Bluebells at Stansted, Kent,* watercolor. Christopher Wood Gallery, London
Opposite: *Ernest Arthur Rowe* (1863–1922), *Bowling Green, Berkeley Castle,* watercolor, 1901. Author's Collection

William Morris would be surprised to learn that he played a considerable role in house and garden design dynamics of the early twentieth century. His first biographer, J. W. Mackail, observed that while Morris always prided himself on his knowledge of gardening, he doubted whether "he was ever seen with a spade in his hands."[1] A passionate poet, calligrapher, manuscript illuminator, printer, embroiderer, entrepreneur, conservationist, utopian thinker, lecturer, writer, and, above all, pattern designer, Morris accomplished more in his lifetime than ten men, dying in his early sixties from sheer exhaustion. Gardens never strayed far from his mind. His two country homes—Red House and Kelmscott Manor—as well as his workshops at Merton Abbey abounded with the flowers, fruits, and birds that formed the core of his firm's famous wallpapers, textiles, and tapestries. Morris's gardens were a testament to his fascination with the Middle Ages and among the earliest examples of the rage for old-fashioned gardens. Morris, in fact, dedicated his life to medieval times, from its romance and visual imagery to the traditional handcrafts and medieval-inspired guilds that made them.

Drawing on the ideas of Gothic Revival architect Augustus Welby Pugin, that the ills of society could be rectified with the spirituality of Gothic art and architecture, Morris embraced medievalism as the model for his life's work. William Morris (1834–1896) spent an idyllic childhood in the country, on the edge of Epping Forest in Essex, where he developed a lifelong passion for all aspects of nature. In the early 1860s, he began designing wallpapers, choosing as his vocabulary the garden and meadow flowers, fruits, and vines

patterns, "Daisy," "Eyebright," "Fritillary," "Honeysuckle," "Larkspur," and scores of others, attest to his devotion to the natural world.[2]

Upon entering Exeter College, Oxford, in 1853, Morris formed important friendships with Edward Burne-Jones, Dante Gabriel Rossetti, and other artists associated with the Pre-Raphaelite Brotherhood. He also came under the influence of John Ruskin, whose book, *Stones of Venice*, ignited his interest in architecture. During a brief apprenticeship with the architect G. E. Street, Morris met Philip Webb, who became an influential friend and collaborator. Morris's new-found fascination with the Arthurian legend opened up a world of medieval lore and soon found him writing poetry epics, such as *The Defence of Guenevere* (1858), *The Life and Death of Jason* (1867), and *The Earthly Paradise* (1868), the latter a three-volume narrative poem that firmly established his reputation as a poet. In all, he wrote dozens of volumes of prose and poetry.

In 1861 Morris founded "The Firm"—Morris, Marshall, Faulkner and Co.—to produce simple, yet elegant home furnishings such as hand-printed wallpapers, fabrics, furniture, and decorative arts, as an antidote to the machine-made, overly ornate Victorian pieces—vestiges of the Great Exhibition of 1851—that he abhorred. Located at first in London's Red Lion Square and later at 449 Oxford Street, the company's showrooms offered commercial wares designed by Burne-Jones, Webb, Ford Madox Brown, William De Morgan, and other artists.[3] Morris's frustration at finding acceptable furnishings for his own home sparked his idea for artists, designers, and craftsmen to work together harmoniously to produce attractive decorative products. Morris's vision centered on transforming prevailing ideas about decorating houses with overwrought goods to simpler, well-designed objects that harkened back to England of the Middle Ages. His dictum—"Have nothing in your houses that you do not know to be useful or believe to be beautiful"—became the guiding

Joseph Pennell (1857–1926), *The Enchanted Doorway (Merton Abbey)*, ink drawing, 1886. Author's Collection

Overleaf:
Philip Webb, *Red House, Bexleyheath, Kent*, 2003

light of his personal mission.[4] The fledgling firm's commission in 1867 to decorate the Green Dining Room at the South Kensington Museum (now the Victoria and Albert Museum, London) set them on their way. In its heyday, the firm produced an exhaustive range of wallpapers, fabrics, tapestries, carpets, furniture, tiles, stained glass, and metalwork, all with characteristic medieval-inspired floral designs.[5] The venture eventually foundered due to the harsh realities of business economics. In a letter to an American admirer in 1884, Morris acknowledged that even though the manner of work done in the Middle Ages was the *only* way, reality proved that it was impossible "in this profit-grinding society."[6]

In later years, Morris turned his energies to socialism, becoming a passionate advocate and lecturer, much to the astonishment of his friends and family. His utopian romance, *News from Nowhere*, describing his beloved home and garden at Kelmscott Manor, was published in 1891, the same year that Morris founded his final enterprise, the Kelmscott Press. Named after Kelmscott House, his home in Hammersmith, Kelmscott Press produced some fifty books, designed and produced by the leading artists of the day, and still considered the apogee of book arts. The sumptuous *Works of Geoffrey Chaucer*, printed on vellum with a decorative cover, was published in 1896, the same year that Morris died.

In the end, Morris's legacy as a pattern designer outlasted his reputation as a poet and socialist; many of the individual patterns remain in production today. His reverence for old buildings, traditional crafts, and the beauty of the English countryside inspired generations of followers, among them Gertrude Jekyll, Ernest Gimson and the Barnsley brothers, Robert Lorimer, C.F.A. Voysey, and M. H. Baillie Scott, who would form the nucleus of the Arts and Crafts Movement. Each designer would leave his own distinctive mark upon architecture and garden design of the period.

William Morris's thoughts on gardens and flowers can be found in some of his writings and not suprisingly he had strong opinions upon the subject. He railed against the popularity of florists' flowers, with all their natural traits bred out of them. "When the florists fell upon the rose [which Morris regarded as the queen of flowers]. . . they strove for size and got it, a fine specimen of a florist's rose being about as big as a moderate Savoy cabbage." They "improved" the scent, but "missed the very essence of the rose's being. . . . they threw away the exquisite subtilty of form, delicacy of texture, and sweetness of color."[7] He also cautioned against double flowers and other tokens of artificiality, such as carpet-bedding ("an aberration of the human mind"), as well as the misuse of

plant curiosities that were more appropriate for botanical gardens than home gardens. He also had definite ideas about the use of color in gardens. "Flowers in masses are mighty strong color, and if not used with a great deal of caution are very destructive to pleasure in gardening," he wrote. Some flowers, such as scarlet geraniums and yellow calceolaria, were simply "bad" and when planted profusely showed that "even flowers can be thoroughly ugly."[8]

Writing in 1879, Morris presaged ideas later promoted by other reformers, notably William Robinson and Gertrude Jekyll. Morris's ideas about the essence of a garden, rather than his thoughts about flowers, provided a credo for garden design theory that spilled over into the early 1900s. In *Hopes and Fears for Art*, Morris wrote:

> Large or small, it should look both orderly and rich. It should be well fenced from the outside world. It should by no means imitate either the wilfulness or the wildness of Nature, but should look like a thing never to be seen except near a house. It should, in fact, look like a part of the house. It follows from this that no private pleasure-garden should be very big, and a public garden should be divided and made to look like so many flower-closes in a meadow, or a wood, or amidst the pavement.[9]

Morris's ideas about domestic architecture, interior design, and gardens coalesced at Red House, his country home near Bexleyheath, Kent. Designed by Philip Webb in 1859, it was the architect's first independent architectural commission and a new home for Morris and his bride, Jane Burden, whom Morris and Rossetti "discovered" in Oxford. A brooding beauty, with masses of dark, wavy hair, Jane was immortalized in Rossetti's paintings. The couple lived at Red House for only five years before Morris was forced to sell it after running into financial difficulties that jeopardized his firm.

Today Red House symbolizes the values that Morris honored most: honesty and beauty. It is also considered the first modern country house, representative of a new approach to house and garden design. Sited in an orchard and meadow, the house and garden are inseparable. "Red House garden, with its long grass walks, its midsummer lilies and autumn sunflowers, its wattled rose-trellises inclosing richly-flowered square garden plots, was then as unique as the house it surrounded," wrote Mackail in 1899.[10] Fiona MacCarthy, Morris's modern biographer, has suggested that the garden was even more influential than the house.[11] May Morris, the Morrises' younger daughter, remembered "the garden that graced this pleasant home [as] characteristic, so happily

Walter Crane (1845–1915), *Tea at Red House,* watercolor. Private Collection

English in its sweetness and freshness, with its rose-hedges and lavender and rosemary borderings to the flower-beds, its alley and bowling green, and the orchard-walks among the apple-trees."[12] Another observer described the garden as "vividly picturesque and uniquely original. . . divided into many squares, hedged with sweet-briar or wild rose, each enclosure with its own particular show of flowers."[13]

This medieval-inspired pleasure garden, filled with gnarled old fruit trees and a subtle selection of simple flowers, was a far cry from the typical parterre gardens of late-Victorian-era estates filled with the vividly colored annuals that Morris loathed. In contrast, the garden at Red House harkened back to a flowery medieval *hortus conclusus*, with enclosure hedges or trellises, straight paths, and profusions of traditional herbs, flowers, and fruits. Such gardens served as a source of inspiration for the firm's renowned tapestries with their minutely detailed floral background. Morris's garden was basically a large square, subdivided into four spaces surrounded by wattle fence, similar to those depicted in medieval illuminated books. It was an earthly paradise, an oasis meant for practicality, enjoyment, and seclusion, rather than ostentatious display.

Red House was profoundly influential in its time, inspiring Gertrude Jekyll, for example, in the design of the interiors of her home at Munstead Wood nearly forty years later. Hermann Muthesius stated that Red House stood "at the threshold of the development of the modern English house," while Rossetti thought it more of a poem than a house.[14] A picturesque Gothic cottage, built of red brick laid in English Bond, with a steeply sloping roof and pointed gables, the exterior belies its light and airy interiors. Behind the small-paned windows lay white-washed walls, exposed brick, red-tiled floors, plain rush-seated chairs, painted cupboards, and all the handmade furnishings that would inspire the formation of the firm. In all, it was living proof of Morris's insatiable thirst for design reform in the domestic arts.

Red House is also remarkable because the house and garden were conceived as an integral unit. A romantic retreat, the house nestles into a surrounding orchard with hedged enclosures demarking the boundaries of the garden. As Mackail remarked, "The building had been planned with such care that hardly a tree in the orchard had to be cut down; apples fell in at the windows as they stood open on hot autumn nights."[15] **Roses** clambered up the side of the house and Webb's fanciful well house with its conical red-tiled roof, which gives so much character to Red House, solidified the relationship between house and garden.[16] Surrounded by trellises covered with roses, white jasmine, and honeysuckle, the well court became a fragrant enclosure where the family and friends could enjoy their afternoon tea. Webb's detailed drawing of the trellis in the original plans for Red House may have inspired Morris's earliest wallpaper design, "The Trellis," in November 1862, for which Webb drew the birds.[17] Even though the outlines of Morris's garden and some of the original fruit trees still survive, the essence of Morris's paradise garden can best be appreciated in the company's legacy of pattern designs and tapestries.

William Morris and Philip Webb, *The Trellis*, wallpaper, 1864. Victoria and Albert Museum, London

POMONA

After leaving Red House, followed by years of living in smoke-choked London, Morris was again able to satisfy his yearnings for a summer place in the country. In 1871 he found an old house about thirty miles from Oxford on the upper reaches of the Thames that would become synonymous with Morris's ideals. Located in a tiny village near Lechlade, Kelmscott Manor is a late-sixteenth-century Tudor manor house, built of gray limestone, with roofs covered in heavy stone slates, and a picturesque farm enclosure replete with a dovecote.[18] He acquired the lease in June that year, but never actually owned the house.[19] It has been said that Morris wanted the house as a love nest for his wife and her lover, Rossetti. Nonetheless, Morris reminisced lovingly about Kelmscott in 1895, remarking on what went into the making of an old house "grown up out of the soil" and the lives of those who lived there before him. He extolled the "sense of delight of meadow and acre and wood and river . . . a liking for making materials serve one's turn . . . and a little grain of sentiment."[20]

In his pithy comments about gardens, he observed that "Many a good house both old and new is marred by the vulgarity and stupidity of its garden, so that one is tormented by having to abstract in one's mind the good building from the nightmare of 'horticulture' which surrounds it." Not so at Kelmscott, where "the garden, divided by old clipped yew hedges, is quite unaffected and very pleasant."[21] In a letter to his mother, Rossetti spoke of the garden as "a perfect paradise."[22] The walled garden was filled with flowers familiar from his pattern designs, and beyond there was a meadow filled with bluebells, apple blossoms, and birdsong, rooks in the elm trees, blackbirds in the garden, and doves on the roof.

The most memorable evocation of Kelmscott is in the closing chapters of *News From Nowhere*, when the wayfayer journeys by riverboat from Hampton Court to Kelmscott:

> . . . my hand raised the latch of a door in the wall, and we stood presently on a stone path which led up to the old house. . . . My companion gave a sigh of pleased surprise and enjoyment. . . for the garden between the wall and the house was redolent of the June flowers, and the roses were rolling over one another with that delicious super-abundance of small, well-tended gardens which at first sight takes away all thought from the beholder save that of beauty.[23]

The garden was to be savored both inside and outside. From one of the rooms of Kelmscott one could "catch a glimpse of the Thames clover meadows and the pretty elm-crowned hill over in Berkshire."[24] If you sat in another place

Marie Spartali Stillman
(1844–1927), *Kelmscott Manor*,
watercolor. Private Collection

Opposite:
Edward Burne-Jones
(1833–98), *Pomona*,
tapestry made by Morris and
Company, c. 1885. Victoria
and Albert Museum, London

you could admire the sharp turn of the gables (the house has seventeen), the stone barn, sheds, and the dovecote. Today those same amenities await the visitor at Kelmscott Manor, although the interiors are not arranged as they were in Morris's day; they were, in fact, quite spartan. Morris thought that Kelmscott embodied the best of England, its countryside, architecture, and gardens.

William Morris, who died in October 1896 from "simply being William Morris," is buried nearby in the Kelmscott churchyard. One hopes that the house and garden brought him much pleasure in his lifetime. His workshops at Merton Abbey, on the River Wandle in Surrey, had equally pleasant surroundings. "His factory [was] a scene of cheerful, uncramped industry, where toil looks like pleasure, where flowers are blooming in windows, and sunshine and fresh air brighten the faces of artist and mechanic." Roses clambered up the ruined abbey walls and a kitchen garden was filled with wild strawberries and plants used for dyes for his textiles.[25] But Red House and Kelmscott Manor above all laid the foundations for the Arts and Crafts approach to home and garden-making, namely the essential relationship between house and garden and the reverence for vernacular building arts.

Kelmscott Manor, Gloucestershire, 1986

Chapter 3 | The Lure of the Cotswolds. The Cotswolds, a region in the West Country noted for its hidden valleys and the distinctive soft, gray limestone used in its buildings, is still a mecca for the Arts and Crafts Movement. Because the Cotswolds were both remote and economically depressed, due to the removal of its once-flourishing wool industry to the north, its sleepy villages and trove of medieval and Tudor stone buildings remained undisturbed, only to be rediscovered in the nineteenth century. William Morris, whose Kelmscott Manor was situated just on the edge of the Cotswolds, reveled in the region's old buildings, traditional crafts, and natural beauty. He, in turn, inspired several architects and designers to move to the Cotswolds to set up workshops practicing some of the local crafts.

In 1884, Morris urged Ernest Gimson (1864–1919), a young man from Leicester who had attended one of his lectures, to become an architect. Armed with a letter of introduction from Morris, Gimson went to work in Sedding's London office, and while there met fellow architect Ernest Barnsley (1863–1926), from Birmingham, as well as his younger brother, Sidney Barnsley (1865–1926), who was in Shaw's office. They all became fast friends, sharing living quarters in London and imbuing themselves in the world of Arts and Crafts, with Morris and Company's showrooms next door to Sedding's office.

According to his biographer, Gimson's gospel was that of William Morris, "of healthy employment for all in making useful and beautiful things or productive agriculture, giving everyone an intelligent interest in their work, time to do it as well as might be, with reasonable leisure time for other interests."[1] Following Morris's recommendation to learn manual skills, Gimson began making rush-seated ladderback chairs, which became a staple of his later workshops. Gimson also became interested in reviving the long-lost art of plasterwork, studying examples in old manor houses. True to Gimson's style, he adapted, rather than copied, antique examples, using floral elements, such as roses, honeysuckle, dianthus, lilies, strawberry plants, and, in later years, his signature squirrels and oak leaves.[2] The Barnsley brothers took up cabinetmaking and woodworking, and all three routinely exhibited their work at the annual venues of the Arts and Crafts Exhibition Society in London.

Topiary at Pinbury Park, Sapperton, Gloucestershire, 1993

After several years devoted to travel (Sidney Barnsley toured Greece in 1888 with Robert Weir Schultz, another important Arts and Crafts architect) or building houses in the Midlands, they became gripped by the romantic notion of living and working in the country.[3] With their families in tow, they removed to the Cotswolds in 1893 to begin earning their livings along the lines dictated by Morris. They were among the first of Morris's disciples to set up workshops in the country. In 1902, Charles R. Ashbee's (1863–1942) Guild of Handicraft, founded in London in the 1880s as a result of the Arts and Crafts Exhibition Society, moved to Chipping Campden, where it continued to produce its distinctive metalwork and furniture until 1907, when it foundered due to competition from companies such as Liberty's.[4]

Gimson and the Barnsleys specialized in a new type of furniture and decorative arts that drew heavily on traditional country models without replicating them. They were renowned for their high level of craftsmanship and their exclusive use of native woods. In their workshops, first at Pinbury Park and later at Daneway House in Sapperton, most of the wares were executed by local cabinetmakers. In addition to their furnishings, which were much in demand, Gimson and the Barnsleys also undertook select architectural commissions, ranging from repairing old buildings to designing new cottages.[5] Their architectural work, which was characterized by a respect for vernacular traditions, use of local building materials, and an affinity for the surrounding landscape, elicited much praise. As one critic wrote in 1909, they "are among the leaders of the school that is seeking to create an original and living style in architecture."[6]

Their fledgling efforts caught the eye of Lord Bathurst, who leased them his summer home at Pinbury Park, with magnificient views over the Sapperton Vale, provided they would repair the old Jacobean house From 1894 until 1901, the families lived together at Pinbury where they established the first of their furniture-making workshops. Under Ernest Barnsley's direction, a wing was added to the house, the ceiling plastered by Gimson, and other improvements were made. At the same time, they refurbished two terraced gardens, one near the house and enclosed by a low dry-stone wall, and the other on a lower level, adjacent to an ancient yew allée. They added a simple, yet elegant stone summerhouse in one corner of the enclosure and lined the garden with clipped topiaries.[7] They would adapt all these elements in their later, more renowned work. When Lord Bathurst returned to take up residence in the newly improved Pinbury Park, he generously gave each of the families land in Sapperton to build its own house. Each house was different and a highly individualistic expression of its designer.

Ernest Barnsley, who was the most outgoing of the three personalities, selected an old cottage dating from approximately 1800, up a steep lane from the village church and commanding a breathtaking view over the vale. Naming it **Upper Dorvel House,** he added two wings to the cottage, carefully marrying the new with the old by adhering to local Cotswold building traditions. Furnished throughout with products of their workshop, the house has a main hall embellished with Gimson's plasterwork ceiling and decorative friezes in floral motifs. Meandering, low stone enclosure walls define the confines of the property, and nestled between the entry drive and the house is small formal garden terrace. Laid out as a rectangular room, an extension of the house, it is "furnished" with neatly clipped boxwood shrubs and simple flower beds. As H. Avray Tipping, *Country Life*'s architecture critic, wrote, "the charm of the little garden makes us pause without. It at once gives the impression that it is right; that it fulfils the particular requirement; that it is of the shape, size, material and construction needed at this special spot. . . . This enclosure. . . is the requisite semi-formal link between the straight lines of the building and the tumbled Cotswold landscape."[8] What Barnsley achieved at Upper Dorvel House—the simple configuration, use of local materials, and intimate relationship with the house—was the essence of an Arts and Crafts garden that would be emulated by many other designers.

Ernest Barnsley, *Upper Dorvel House, Sapperton, Gloucestershire,* 1989
Frederick L. Griggs (1879–1938), *Leasowes,* engraving, 1922 (from Lethaby, Powell, and Griggs, *Ernest Gimson, His Life and Work,* 1924). Author's Collection

Gimson built himself a new L-shaped cottage, named Leasowes, with rough stone walls and a thatched roof. His house, which reflects his exacting requirements and the effects he wished to produce, is conspicuous for its absence of ornamentation, an austerity that marks his furniture designs. Described as "a thinker, an explorer, a teacher," Gimson was the more reflective of the three and passionately committed to the ideals of the Arts and Crafts Movement, embracing simplicity, utlilty, and respect for materials in all of his work.[9] In the living room, a plain whitewashed ceiling with oak beams, thick stone walls, and a large open hearth provide an atmosphere that one critic called "a temple of elegance and refinement."[10] Like Upper Dorvel House, the grounds are enclosed by low drystone walls, with an extraordinary stone dovecote at the entry gate. The finely crafted rubblestone wall and towering dovecote caught the eye of *Country Life,* which included a photograph of it in Lawrence Weaver's *Small Country Houses of To-Day* in 1912. The dove-

Ernest Gimson, *Leasowes, Sapperton, Gloucestershire,* 1989
Sidney Barnsley's *dovecote at Beechanger, Sapperton, Gloucestershire,* 1989

cote's rustic charm symbolizes the creativity of architectural detailing during the Arts and Crafts era. Gertrude Jekyll and Lawrence Weaver praised Gimson's naturalistic pool at Stoneywell Cottage, near Leicester, where the margin carefully followed the natural contours of the ground. "Mr. Gimson," they wrote, "has shown an appreciation of the character of the site by making the pool accord in its rough simplicity with the attractive, roughly-built cottage."[11]

Sidney Barnsley, who was more apt to work on his own, rather than provide designs for furniture to be made by crafts-men, built himself a small, rustic stone cottage with thick stone slabs on the roof. Like Gimson's cottage, Barnsley's Beechanger has an extraordinary dovecote rising from the stone wall like a lighthouse looming up at sea. Sidney was involved in architectural work on two old Cotswold manor houses, both with noteworthy gardens. In the 1920s, he remodeled Combend Manor, a seventeenth-century house in Elkstone, and laid out a garden, loosely configured in a series of terraces near the house, and a naturalistic pond garden farther away near the orchard. Characteristically, the terrace gardens were enclosed by low drystone walls, with a stone summerhouse in one corner, and several archways, one with a dovecote at the top.

In July 1925, Gertrude Jekyll prepared planting plans for the pond garden and the herbaceous borders at Combend Manor. Her introduction to Sidney Barnsley may have come from their mutual friend, the architect Robert Weir Schultz.[12] Jekyll, who was then eighty-one years old, sent detailed planting plans for the garden, based primarily on the survey plan pro-

Above:
Sidney Barnsley, *Long border
and stone summerhouse at
Combend Manor, Elkstone,
Gloucestershire, 1989*

Opposite:
Sidney Barnsley, *Garden arch-
way with dovecote at Combend
Manor, Elkstone, Gloucestershire,
1993*

Overleaf:
**Sidney Barnsley and
Norman Jewson,** *Cotswold
Farm, Duntisbourne Abbots,
Gloucestershire, 1989*

vided by Barnsley. The pond garden, with drifts of ferns,
shrub roses, and naturalized groupings of bulbs in the grass,
did not go forward, although there is a similar water garden
there today. Her recommendations for the double herbaceous
borders leading to the summerhouse are thought to have
been implemented. At this time in her life, Jekyll worked
almost entirely from her exhaustive memory of plants, providing her signature, but predictable, groupings of favorite perennials. Her mind was still exceptionally acute in sounding out
overall design improvements, but a number of her recommendations for architectural embellishments for Barnsley's plan,
including a pergola to frame the view across the valley, were
nixed by the architect.[13]

At Cotswold Farm, a seventeenth-century house in Duntisbourne Abbots, not far from Cirencester, Sidney Barnsley
added two wings in 1926 for Sir John and Lady Birchall. After
Barnsley's death later that year, Norman Jewson (1884–1975),
who originally came to Gimson's office in 1907, made further
improvements to Cotswold Farm. He laid out extensive terraced gardens on the hillside in 1938, replete with a characteristic stone summerhouse in the lower garden. His stone terraces, connected by a series of steep staircases, gave architectural bones to the garden. In later years, the Birchalls' daugh-
ter-in-law transformed Jewson's garden into a horticultural

paradise, with the introduction of rare trees, shrubs, and herbaceous perennials in the best tradition of English garden-making. On the upper terrace, overlooking the unspoiled valley, a group of columnar box topiaries lend the house and garden its unmistakable Cotswold character.[14]

Norman Jewson, who chronicled the work of Gimson and the Barnsleys in his autobiographical memoir, *By Chance I Did Rove*, worked in the traditional Cotswold manner, refurbishing a number of manor houses. Jewson, who set up his own practice in 1919 after working briefly for Gimson, was noted for his exceptional craftsmanship, respect for traditional building techniques, and conservation efforts. As he modestly observed, "I hoped that my buildings would at least have good manners and be able to take their natural place in their surroundings without offence."[15]

In 1925 he purchased Owlpen Manor, a Tudor manor house near Uley, of medieval origin, with sixteenth- and seventeenth-century additions. Jewson spent the next several years carefully repairing it. The interiors are embellished with modeled plasterwork by both Jewson and Gimson, as well as furnishings designed by all and made by teams of local craftsmen.[16] The three asymmetrical bays, each dating from a different era, overlook a rare intact old garden in the foreground and a beautiful valley in the distance. Owlpen folds so naturally into the hill that it gives new meaning to the symbiotic relationship between house and surrounding landscape. The name "Owlpen" (which apparently has nothing to do with owls) implies enclosure.[17]

The old garden had been admired by many travelers, among them Gertrude Jekyll, Vita Sackville-West, and Geoffrey Jellicoe. As Jekyll and Weaver wrote in *Gardens for Small Country Houses*, plans and photographs can never convey "the wealth of incident crowded into an area of little more than half an acre" or "with what modesty the house nestles against the hillside and seeks to hide itself amidst regiments of yews."[18] The yews, in fact, are one of the distinguishing features of the garden. The square Yew Parlour, in Jekyll's day nearly twenty-five feet high and varying from six to ten feet wide, was prob-

Frederick L. Griggs (1879–1938),
Owlpen Manor, etching, 1931.
Courtesy Nicholas and Karin
Mander, Owlpen Manor

Opposite:
Simon Dorrell, *Garden plan
of Owlpen Manor,* 2003

ably planted in the early eighteenth century when the medieval garden was refurbished. The site, which slopes dramatically to the south, is edged with rows of massive yews on the upper slope and along the main garden path to the south. This dramatic view has been memorialized in a Gothic-inspired etching by Frederick L. Griggs, an important artist and sometime architectural associate of Jewson's. In 1927, an American architect commented that the garden "is one of the finest and most satisfying things of its kind anywhere [with] whimsical conceits, such as peacocks and dragons in yew."[19] Although not large in size, the form and planting of the garden is straightforward, yet dramatic.

In 1908 Gimson began work at the Drakestone estate near Stinchcombe, with its incomparable views over the Vale of Berkeley and the Welsh marshes. He got no further than constructing two stone cottages before his clients, Walter and Mabel St. John-Mildmay, replaced him with Oswald P. Milne (1881–1968), a young architect who had been a pupil in Lutyens's office.[20] Drakestone, which nestles into the hill, is

the quintessence of an Arts and Crafts family house It is built of local golden stone, with a stone roof that was a traditional feature of the region. Milne also designed a stone terrace, with walls and stairways leading to the garden, where a double-stairway, built over an arch with a Lutyens-inspired pool underneath, offers an enchanting view to the house. Weaver praised Drakestone as a "good example of the success which comes from the right handling, in the simplest way, of materials beautiful in themselves."[21]

Around 1909 Ernest Barnsley received a commission that would bring a new dimension to the planning of a house and garden. After visiting Rodmarton in 1914, Ashbee exclaimed, "The English Arts and Crafts movement at its best is here— so are the vanishing traditions of the Cotswolds."[22] Claud Biddulph, who had probably spotted Country Life's article on Barnsley's own house in April 1909, asked Barnsley to design a "cottage in the country" that would be at once substantial in size and offer employment to the many local people. His plan was to spend no more than £5,000 per year, but his

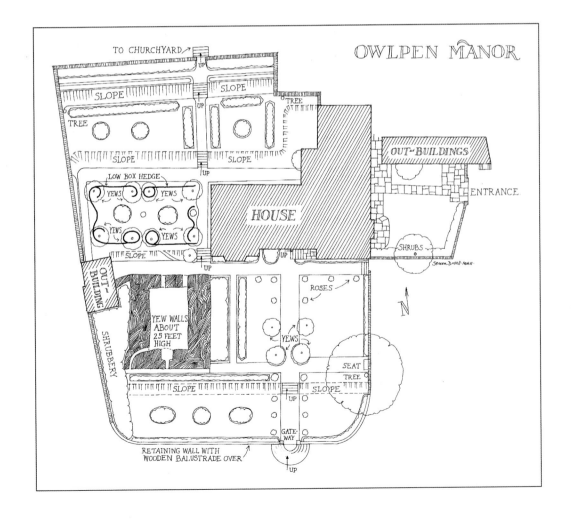

undertaking took until 1929 to complete.[23] During this time the project grew from a small country house to a large manor house. It has been owned by three generations of the same family and, unusually, is in unaltered condition today.

No doubt Biddulph was drawn to Barnsley because of Barnsley's own house (just four miles from Rodmarton), but also for the furnishings produced in the Sapperton workshops. Rodmarton was painstakingly built by hand from local materials—stone from a local quarry and timber felled on the estate—by local laborers and furnished throughout with decorative furnishings designed by the Barnsleys that were made in their workshops or on site. Jewson designed most of the decorative leadwork, featuring flora and fauna motifs. Conceived to look like a series of cottages on a village street,

with five gables on the front and five on the garden side of the main house, Rodmarton gives a nod to the old, but avoids line-by-line imitation

Barnsley provided the overall garden plan, laid out as a series of outdoor rooms, each enclosed by low stone walls or clipped hedges, leaving most of the details to the head gardener, William Scrubey. The ingenious series of interconnecting gardens, ranging from formal near to the house to informal farther afield, is based on the theories set forth in Sedding's *Garden-Craft Old and New*. This is not surprising, since Ernest Barnsley initially trained with Sedding in London. The gardens encompass most of the dominant theories of garden design at the time, from Robinson in the wilder parts to Jekyll in the more formal areas.

Above:
Oswald Milne, *Garden stair cases at Drakestone Manor,* 1919. Country Life Picture Library

Opposite:
Oswald Milne, *Drakestone Manor, Stinchcombe, Gloucestershire,* 1989

The gardens lying to the west of the house have been designed to maximize the view across the Marlborough Downs from the south façade. The terrace on the south face is treated as the most formal "room," with clipped yew hedges and Portuguese laurels.[24] Adjacent rooms include a troughery and topiary garden, decorated with stone feeding troughs collected from the farm and planted with alpines, and a winter garden, now planted with a pleached lime allée. Below the terrace, abutting the meadow, is a rustic stone pergola, covered in flame-red *Vitis cognettiae* in the autumn. On axis with the terrace gardens is one of the most dramatic sequences of the garden, a double-bordered walk, enclosed by high hedges, with a stone summerhouse to denote the end of the vista. From the summerhouse, one can gaze across the borders to the house. The borders, which were refurbished in the 1990s, are thirteen feet wide and planted in large drifts reminiscent of Jekyll's style. A large kitchen garden lies behind one side of the borders, while on the other are a series of rooms, including a tennis court and a swimming pool, each suitably enclosed with high hedges. Even the wilder components of the garden—a rockery, croquet lawn, and orchard— are carefully delineated within geometric confines. The hornbeam allée, underplanted with wild cow parsley and combining formality and informality, is just one of the many incidents in the garden. The gardens at Rodmarton have only increased in their beauty as they have matured. At once there is a sense of privacy, enclosure, subtlety, and an inordinate attention to detail, just as in the house. In many ways Rodmarton stands as the supreme example of the vision of Ernest Gimson, the Barnsleys, and their associates in the Cotswolds.

Above:
Ernest Barnsley, Rodmarton Manor, Gloucestershire, 1989

Opposite top:
Ernest Barnsley, Herbaceous borders at Rodmarton Manor, 1989

Opposite bottom:
Simon Dorrell, Garden plan of Rodmarton Manor, 2003

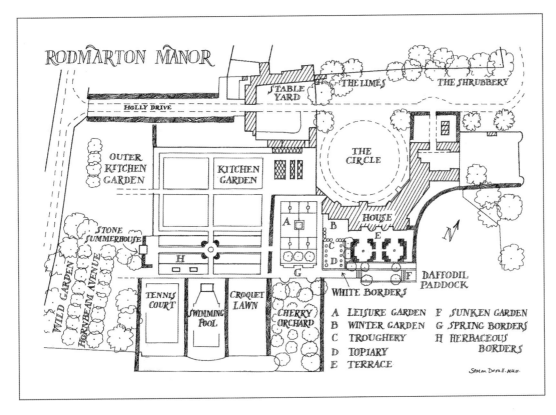

RODMARTON MANOR

THE LIMES   THE SHRUBBERY

STABLE YARD

HOLLY DRIVE

THE CIRCLE

OUTER KITCHEN GARDEN

KITCHEN GARDEN

HOUSE

STONE SUMMERHOUSE

A   B
E
C
D
G
F   DAFFODIL PADDOCK

H

WHITE BORDERS

WILD GARDEN

HORNBEAM AVENUE

TENNIS COURT

SWIMMING POOL

CROQUET LAWN

CHERRY ORCHARD

A LEISURE GARDEN   F SUNKEN GARDEN
B WINTER GARDEN   G SPRING BORDERS
C TROUGHERY   H HERBACEOUS
D TOPIARY   BORDERS
E TERRACE

Simon Dorrell · MMII ·

More than any other publication of the period, *The Studio* magazine reveals how artists and architects actually envisioned gardens. Founded in 1893 by Charles Holme, an art connoisseur and latter-day owner of Morris's Red House, *The Studio* celebrated the new approach to art and design that emerged at the end of the nineteenth century.[1] It appealed to the younger generation of art-lovers and artists who had tired of the late Victorian era's stale academic approach to art and embraced the current House Beautiful aesthetic.[2] Adopting the motto "Use and Beauty," the magazine was singular for recognizing applied art and craftsmanship as the equal of fine art. Its coverage included jewelry, metalwork, embroidery, photography, and book arts as well as domestic architecture, interior decoration, and garden design.[3]

In addition to its unparalleled coverage of all the arts, one of the reasons that *The Studio* was so successful was its exceptional illustrations. Its covers—the initial one was designed by Aubrey Beardsley and others by C.F.A. Voysey—lent a distinctive graphic identity to the magazine. Early issues included facsimiles of lithographs made especially for the magazine by James McNeill Whistler and other fashionable artists. *The Studio*'s reviews of the Arts and Crafts Exhibition Society's annual venues and its sponsorship of design competitions appealed to up-and-coming architects, artists, and designers. Extensive coverage of trends in Europe and America gave birth to *The International Studio*, for many years a mainstay of art schools abroad. *The Studio* also published volumes devoted to individual artists and themes, annual yearbooks of decorative arts, gardening annuals, and a formidable range of books, including *The Gardens of England,* edited by Holme.[4]

The Studio's attractive color renderings of houses and gardens encapsulate the versatility and creativity of garden design from the architectural viewpoint. Even though many of these renderings were romanticized

C.F.A. Voysey, cover for *The Studio,* 1893. Author's Collection.

visions of gardens, they were always rich in imagination and detail. The evocative rendering of High Moss, near Keswick, is an excellent example of the type of designs that architects were producing at the time. Designed by William Henry Ward, the fanciful garden at High Moss, a storybook double-gabled, whitewashed cottage, lacks the finesse of more practiced designers.[5] The walled enclosure, anchored by twin garden houses, with paved and topiary gardens surrounded by high, clipped hedges, is more suited to a small Elizabethan manor house than a vernacular-style Lakeland cottage.[6] A scheme for a house in Barnsley shows a linear hedge with arched openings separating the front lawn from the geometric garden enclosures. Parterre beds, planted with rose or peony standards and clipped yews in one area, and a sundial garden in the other, offer pleasant, but undistinguished outdoor spaces.

The Studio was among the first to champion Voysey (whose work was featured in the first issue), Baillie Scott, Charles Mallows, Charles Rennie Mackintosh, and other architects associated with the new art. Most of the architects hailed by The Studio were largely ignored by Country Life magazine, founded four years later to promote upper-class country living. Country Life championed architects such as Edwin Lutyens and Robert Lorimer, whose clients sought houses steeped in vernacular traditions, rather than the artistic homes favored by The Studio.

The Scottish architect Charles Rennie Mackintosh (1868–1928) was one of the most original architects to emerge in the mid-1890s. He was described by Muthesius as "an architect to his fingertips [with a] strong architectural sense" that prevailed in his idiosyncratic buildings and furnishings.[7] Although Mackintosh's early sensibilities were founded in the Arts and Crafts philosophy, his work rapidly transcended the insularity of his English contemporaries. Mackintosh and his circle, including the Macdonald sisters and Herbert MacNair (all based at the Glasgow School of Art), gave birth to the Glasgow style in their revolutionary display at the Arts and Crafts Exhibition Society in 1896.[8] The group's distinctive embroideries, metalwork, posters, and furniture,

later shown in international exhibitions, would have far-reaching influence on modern design.[9] The Macdonald sisters'
highly stylized flowers and elongated female figures in their
gesso panels and stained glass formed the decorative base in
their numerous Glasgow commissions, including interiors for
four tearooms designed by Mackintosh.

Mackintosh's architectural work was widely applauded
abroad. His entry for the 1901 German-sponsored *Haus eines
Kunstfreundes* (House for an Art Lover) competition signaled
his unusually fertile approach to design. Mackintosh's masterpiece, the Glasgow School of Art, and several country houses
are legendary. His passion for decoration, whether flower
studies, landscapes, or textiles painted in his last years when
his architectural commissions diminished, all attest to his
unique vision.[10]

Along with the Glasgow School of Art, Hill House is his
best-known and preserved work. He received the commission
from the prominent Glasgow publisher Walter Blackie in
1902, shortly after being made partner in the architectural
firm Honeyman, Keppie, and Mackintosh.

Mackintosh's charge was to design a country house in Helensburgh, Dunbartonshire, on the top of a hill overlooking the Firth of Clyde. When **Mackintosh** handed Blackie the plans, he wrote: "Here is the house. It is not an Italian villa, or English Mansion House, Swiss Chalet, or a Scotch Castle. It is a Dwelling House."[11] His design was vaguely Scottish baronial, but the light gray stucco exterior, with unadorned gables and chimneys and asymmetrical windows with minimal dressings, signaled a revolutionary approach. The interior spaces are dramatic and unconventional, with stark dark-stained wood on the main floor and ethereal white bedrooms with elegant rose and lavender-colored fittings upstairs. The decorations, designed in collaboration with his wife, Margaret Macdonald Mackintosh, ranged from his signature geometric furniture to striking metal-and-glass light fixtures. One hundred years later the house is still awesome, rising up like a phoenix on a hillside among more conventional homes.

Above: *Charles Rennie Mackintosh, Hill House, Helensburgh,* 1987
Opposite: *Ornamental dovecote at Hill House,* 1987

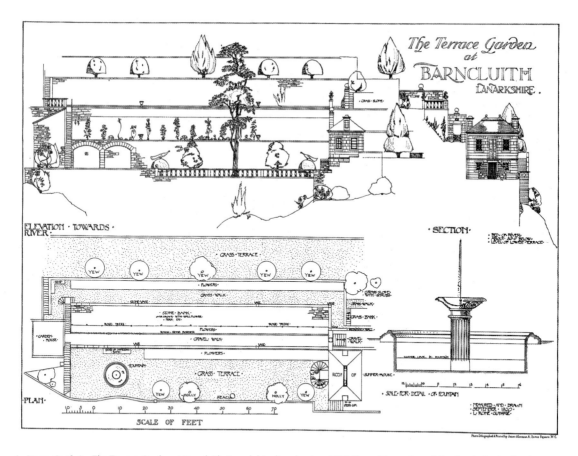

L. Rome Guthrie, *The Terrace Garden at Barncluith, Lanarkshire,* line drawing, 1900 (from Triggs, *Formal Gardens in England and Scotland,* 1902, plate 78). Author's Collection

The garden is rarely mentioned, but Mackintosh's perspectives of the house show how he linked indoor and outdoor spaces through geometry. There are low terrace walls, with espaliered shrubs of impossible form and glittering fruit trees that seem to be on the verge of bursting, and a baronial-style dovecote anchored in one corner. The semicircular entry drive is lined with square-shaped rose standards. U-shaped spy holes on the boundary walls frame the appropriate viewpoints to the house. The garden plan echoed the square motifs used in the furniture and light fixtures in the house. The terrace divided into nine squares resembles an outdoor gameboard for tic-tac-toe, or one of Mackintosh's ebonized tables or metal lighting fixtures.[12]

The contemporary Glasgow architect John James Joass (1868–1952) was the first to address the history and lore of garden design in the pages of *The Studio.* Joass made a case for seventeenth-century formal gardens in Scotland as a worthy prototype for new gardens. Referring to the lengthy debates about the "relative function of the architect and the horticultural artist in regard to garden design," Joass argued that since the Renaissance architects had shown themselves quite capable of designing gardens. The moderate scale of seventeenth-century Scots gardens were excellent models "for everyday application when the pleasaunce is becoming again a part of the English dwelling," he wrote.[13] Old Scots garden enclosures (or pleasances), with their characteristic walls, ornamental detailing, and garden buildings, provided inspiration and vocabulary for Arts and Crafts gardens. Barncluith, a steeply terraced garden overhanging the River Evan in Lanarkshire, is sheltered by long enclosure walls and has fanciful bird topiaries in yew and box, as well as traditional summerhouses. "It is quite unlike anything else," wrote another Scotsman, Robert Lorimer. "It is the most romantic little garden in Scotland."[14] Stobhall, in Perthshire, overlooking the River Tay, is another romantic garden, with a seventeenth-century topiary garden and dwellings dating to the same century.

L. Rome Guthrie, *Stobhall, Perthshire,* line drawing (from Triggs, *Formal Gardens of England and Scotland,* 1902, plate 72). Author's Collection

As envisioned by L. Rome Guthrie, an Arts and Crafts architect who supplied illustrations for Triggs's *Formal Gardens of England and Scotland*, the elegant central sundial and exaggerated yews are a perfect match for the old house.

Even though he was not the first to write about garden design in *The Studio*, Edward Schroeder Prior (1852–1932) summed up the magazine's approach to the decorative aspects of a garden. An important Arts and Crafts architect, Prior "was the most eccentric, intellectual and original pupil in the Shaw office," according to historian Margaret Richardson.[15] A founder member of the Art Workers' Guild and secretary of the Arts and Crafts Exhibition Society, Prior was known for his highly original blending of building materials in two extant projects, The Barn, in Exmouth, Devon, and Home Place, Norfolk.[16] Prior addressed his articles to "garden-makers as artists," outlining the principles, practice, and materials that one needed to grasp. "The garden's immediate connection with the house is manifest," he wrote, reiterating

much that had been first said earlier by Sedding.[17] Prior was critical of the improper use of materials and referred to the "nastiness of the materials of garden-design" and "the present-day vulgarities of commercial material [which need] to be taken into account by the garden-maker."[18] He recommended the creation of an enclosure with hedges or walls, the use of stone for edging paths, and straight lines for laying out flower beds. "Of course in practice irregular slopes and irregular boundaries are the common lot, but let not the garden-maker be discouraged. Out of such material his art grows," he concluded.[19]

Among *The Studio*'s writers, Charles Edward Mallows (1864–1915) had the most significant impact in defining the essential guidelines of good garden design for Arts and Crafts architects. Mallows possessed an artist's eye for composition and appropriateness, and regardless of the size of the houses he designed, they always appeared unpretentious, in keeping with the theories of the Arts and Crafts Movement. Although little remains of Mallows's built work, his renderings for schemes, both real and imaginary, distill the essence of architectural gardening at its best.[20]

Lawrence Weaver and Gertrude Jekyll praised Mallows in *Gardens for Small Country Houses*, singling out one of his houses for the "close connection of house and garden," the underlying premise of their book.[21] Typical Mallows's schemes employ a simple sunken garden, sometimes with a central pool, and architectural devices such as covered archways to connect house and garden. Brackenston, in Pembury, Kent, designed around 1904 for the Reverend R.F.W. Molesworth, has a straightforward layout of terraces, with low walls and a simple pergola enclosing the garden. He possessed an unusually observant eye for paving, steps, pergolas, and other architectural detailing, all designed to a good scale. Together with his pupil, F. L. Griggs, Mallows wrote numerous articles on architectural gardening for *The Studio* between 1908 and 1910 that introduced the nuances of garden design to the younger generation. They served as a forum for Mallows's own work and theories.

Frederick Landseer Griggs (1879–1938), who was known for his brooding etchings of rural cottages and the English countryside, was one of the leaders of the Arts and Crafts Movement.[22] Associated with the Cotswold School, he counted Charles Ashbee, Philip Webb, Ernest Gimson, and the Barnsley brothers among his friends. Although he trained as an architect, it was his talent as an architectural draftsman and etcher that brought him considerable renown. His etchings of imaginary medieval buildings form the core of his artistic talent, but he also illustrated numerous books, including garden memoirs.[23]

In their articles for *The Studio*, Mallows and Griggs captured the essence of the symbiotic nature of gardens and architecture in both words and pictures. "The happy union of house and garden in architectural design," they wrote, emerged in sixteenth-century England as the result of designers considering "reasonableness and order" as necessary components to all good architecture. Mallows paid tribute to Sedding, whose principles of twenty years earlier had finally seen the demise of the "landscape man" in favor of architectural gardening.[24] Flagged walks flanked by high hedges and other equally simple devices inspired by old manor house gardens, could be used to great effect in new gardens for smaller houses, he advised, echoing the words of Sedding. But even the best of garden planning, they argued, could be spoiled by the faulty arrangement or lack of scale in the detailing. Decorative features, such as lead figures, sundials, and balustrades "should always be judged on the site and never left to be settled by designs on paper, however carefully they may be worked out."[25] In general, their recommendations for garden design were sensible, if not self-effacing.

Charles E. Mallows, Design for Brackenston, Pembury, Kent, pencil drawing by F. L. Griggs, 1904. RIBA Library Drawings Collection, London

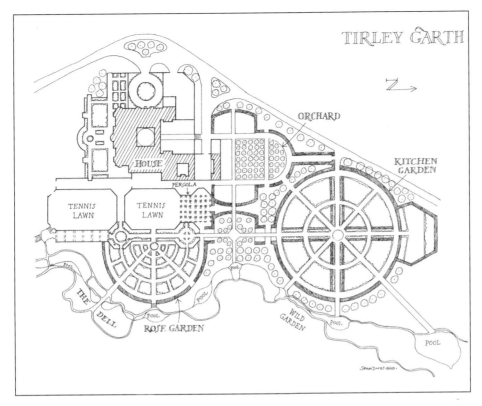

Simon Dorrell, *Garden plan for Tirley Garth,* 2003

The two most complete examples of Mallows's work are Craig-y-Parc, in Pentyrch, near Cardiff, and Tirley Garth, both of which bring to life his ideas about garden planning. Designed in 1913 for Thomas Evans, a colliery owner in Wales, Craig-y-Parc is a double-gabled house, with a cloister court connecting the two wings, overlooking a formal terraced garden. A small rose garden adjacent to one wing and a lily garden on the other serve as outdoor rooms. From the long flight of steps leading down to the lawn enclosed by low stone walls, there is a grand view of the countryside of rural South Wales. Woodland gardens on the entrance side of the house provide the requisite balance between informality and formality.

Tirley Garth, near Taporley, Cheshire, is a gracious country house, originally commissioned by Bryan Leesmith in 1906, when it was called Tirley Court. It was not completed until 1912 by the second owner, Richard Prestwich, a Manchester textile industrialist. The house, built around a central courtyard, with an enclosed cloister walk serving as part of the terrace, is a grander version of Craig-y-Parc. The site was selected to take advantage of the superb view across the Cheshire plain.[26]

Tirley Garth also has an outstanding garden, conceptualized for the first client, but not built until 1912. Mallows's sketches, first published in 1908 in *The Studio*, show a strong architectonic conception. When the project finally went forward, Mallows decided to consult with landscape architect Thomas Mawson for recommendations for the plantings. Mallows made skillful use of the different levels of the hillside site, with a circular vegetable garden, encompassing an acre in size, at the uppermost elevation, and a long, linear axis connecting the circular garden with a semicircular rose garden on axis with the house. The paving, steps, and architectural detailing that define each of the levels and garden areas is a tribute to Arts and Crafts sensibilities of utility and beauty as well as an example of "the happy union of house and garden." Tirley Garth still retains Mallows's remarkable hardscaping, along with Mawson's horticultural elements, including impressive sweeps of mature rhododendron plantations. But it is Mallows's visionary perspectives that bring the garden alive as it was in the Arts and Crafts era.

Charles E. Mallows,
Garden Entrance to Tirley Court,
line drawing, 1908 (from *The*
Studio, October 1908). Author's
Collection

Charles E. Mallows,
Tirley Garth, Taporley, Cheshire,
1992

Chapter 5 | Individuality and Imagination.

Of the many architects who created innovative houses and gardens during the Arts and Crafts era, C.F.A. Voysey and M. H. Baillie Scott stand out for their highly identifiable styles and fertile imagination. *The Studio* hailed Baillie Scott as "one of the most individual architects of the present day" and Voysey detailed his philosophy in a tract entitled *Individuality*.[1] Early in their careers, the ideals of the Arts and Crafts Movement helped shape their approach to architecture and design. They furnished their houses with wallpapers, fabrics, and decorations of their own designs as well as provided appropriate gardens for them. Both architects appealed to middle-class clients with artistic leanings, such as artists, writers, and publishers. Baillie Scott had a longer, more successful career than Voysey, attracted an international following, and was able to adapt long after the Arts and Crafts Movement had been eclipsed. Voysey, whose ironclad principles never wavered, saw the demise of his architectural career when he failed to grasp the changes wrought by World War I. Today he is hailed for his imaginative houses and simplistic pattern designs that evoke the carefree, childlike world of a bygone era.

Charles Francis Annesley Voysey (1857–1941) grew up in an unusual household in rural Yorkshire, where his father, the Reverend Charles Voysey, was expelled from the Church of England for questioning church doctrine. Voysey's personal ideology, which suffused all his work, was an odd combination of the puritanism of John Wesley (one of his ancestors) and the Gothic revivalism of Pugin. John Betjeman, the witty poet laureate and editor of *The Architectural Review*, wisely observed that Voysey interpreted in stone and color what the Reverend Voysey had preached.[2]

Voysey was articled for five years to the ecclesiastical architect John Pollard Seddon; his later experience in Devey's office quickened his approach to domestic architecture. After he launched his own practice in the late 1880s, commissions were slow to materialize. He then turned to pattern design at the suggestion of Arthur Heygate Macmurdo, a well-known designer and founder of the Century Guild. Voysey continued to design wallpapers and textiles well into the 1930s, when, as a disillusioned and somewhat bitter man, these activities provided him with a source of income during lean years. In the 1890s, he built some of his best-known houses: Broadleys, Moorcrag, Grey Friars, and New Place.[3]

Known for his idiosyncratic architectural vocabulary of roughcast houses with low, projecting eaves, green slate roofs, and massive buttresses and chimneys, Voysey was one of the most original architects of the era. His houses were economical and efficient—his personal motto was "keep it simple." As Baillie Scott wrote in 1907, just as Voysey's career was beginning to fade, "If one were asked to sum up in a few words the scope and purposes of Mr. Voysey's work, one might say that it consists mainly in the application of serenely sane, practical and rational ideas to home making."[4] Edwin Lutyens praised his originality, "the 'hearted shutters,' the client's profile on a bracket, the absence of accepted forms, the long, sloping, slate-clad roofs, [and] white walls clear and clean! No detail was too small for Voysey's volatile brain."[5]

The Orchard, Voysey's own modest house, best symbolizes his ideal home. "Untrammelled by the intervention of a client," as one critic remarked, the architect did just as he pleased.[6] Located in Chorleywood, in suburban Hertfordshire, it was within easy reach of his London office on the Metropolitan railway line.[7] The exterior is whitewashed rough-cast, with towering chimneys and a green slate roof, while the interiors were predominantly white, with slate floors and turkey-red curtains. Voysey designed every detail, from the carpets and wallpapers to the furniture and the metal fittings on the doors. The overall impression was one of lightness, simplicity, and purpose. Only twenty feet from the village road, the front door to the house was approached through a

straight path bordered by yew hedges. The welcoming doorway, glimpsed through the hedges, had his signature heart-shaped letter-box. Surrounded by a two-acre orchard filled with old apple trees, walnut trees, hollies, and a large cherry tree, The Orchard also had a flower garden filled with roses and birds, which dominate his wallpaper and textile patterns.

Fundamental to an appreciation of Voysey is his duality as an architect and a designer. As a fledgling architect, Voysey presented himself as an artist, wearing clothing of his own design (such as cuffless trousers and jackets without lapels) and donning artistic-looking hats. In his architectural work, he adopted a limited palette of colors, primarily black, white, pale green, and deep red accents. An active member of the Art Workers' Guild, Voysey frequently exhibited his wallpapers, textiles, metalwork, and furniture at the Arts and Crafts Exhibition Society's annual exhibitions in London. His evocative pattern designs and the quaint simplicity of his houses quickly caught the public's attention. In an 1893 interview in *The Studio*, Voysey held the Morrisian line that artists should work in healthy environments and sweep ugliness away (although he disliked Morris personally due to his atheism), but his theories about ornamentation were more specific. "The danger to-day lies in over-decoration," he said, "we lack simplicity and have forgotten repose, and so the relative value of beautiful things is confounded."[8] Perhaps as a rationale for not building houses at the time, he observed that wallpaper could help disguise the ugliness of bad furnishings that he found so prevalent. Although he was an exceptional wallpaper designer, his preferred treatment for walls was, in fact, wood paneling, either stained or polished; in most of his houses wallpaper was generally confined to the bedrooms.

Voysey's patterns portray an imaginary world of birds, trees, animals, and flowers reduced to symbols, unlike Morris's more flowing, detailed patterns. Some of Voysey's designs reveal a darker side to his personality, with a recurring demon figure that also appears in his tiles, gate latches, and sundials, as well as menacing birds and other unsavory characters. His demonesque gargoyle was hailed for its

Opposite top:
C.F.A. Voysey, *The Orchard, Chorleywood, Hertfordshire,* line drawing (from *Studio Special Number,* 1901). Author's Collection

Opposite bottom:
C.F.A. Voysey, *Stag and Swans,* woolen textile, 1899. Victoria and Albert Museum, London

Left:
C.F.A. Voysey, *The Squire's Garden,* wallpaper, 1896. Victoria and Albert Museum, London

"delightfully grotesque quality. . . suggestive of the medieval craftsman" by Jekyll and Weaver in *Gardens for Small Country Houses.*[9] Most of his patterns depict a happy world of song birds, flowers, berries, and fruits, an idealized Garden of Eden, with columnar evergreens interspersed with fruit trees clipped into heart-shaped standards. "The Squire's Garden" is a medieval *hortus conclusus* enclosed by vine-covered trellises and ornamented with potted trees, trees clipped into pyramidal shapes, a pigeoncote, a sundial, peacocks, and garden birds.

Although Voysey is not known as a garden designer, he provided layouts for grounds and gardens in the course of his work, crossing paths with Gertrude Jekyll and Thomas Mawson, who designed gardens for several of his clients.[10] Typically Voysey specified enclosure walls, usually roughcast, as well as garden houses, dovecotes, gates, sundials, and other components that harmonized with the style of the house. These were all practical as well as ornamental features, especially dovecotes, which attracted the all-important birds into the garden.

Watercolor perspectives of Voysey's houses, some prepared by the architect himself, have lush settings that often blend formal flower gardens with more naturalistic areas. For Oakhurst, in Fernhurst, Sussex, Voysey chose a view of the house across a green Robinsonian meadow filled with carpets of scillas and daisies. The long, low house is atypical in form for Voysey, but replete with all his signature details. A stone wall along the embankment accommodates the grade change, while low, clipped hedges with topiaries mark the entrance to the garden. An arch in the back hedge takes its curve from the eyebrow recess

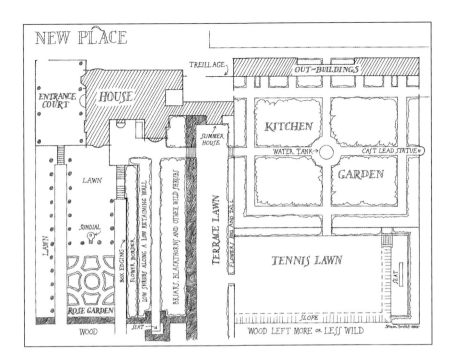

over the garden gate and doorway. The cheerful garden inside the enclosure is filled with climbing roses, hollyhocks, and rose standards, all improbably blooming at the same time as the meadow flowers. The scarlet color serves to highlight the red curtains in the windows and the tile detailing on the house. The garden is a fantasy not unlike those in Voysey's wallpapers and textiles.

The garden at New Place, near Haslemere, Surrey, is a rare survival of his work. Designed in 1897 for Sir Algernon Methuen, founder of the Methuen publishing company and an alpine fancier, the house and garden are considered one of Voysey's most successful. "The mind and heart of the owner," wrote one critic about New Place, "are plainly traceable in the perfect way in which the formal gardens next to the house gradually merge into the informal and wild parts further down the slope."[11] Voysey's initial plan for the grounds carries the notations, "flowers big and tall," "high yew and holly hedge," "briars, blackthorns, and other wild shrubs," and "wood left more or less wild."[12]

The formal garden enclosures are arranged on four ascending levels to accommodate the steeply sloping site and enclosed with low brick walls. A sunken garden on the lowest level, adjoining the main drawing room, has junipers in each corner and a central sundial. The main garden borders, filled with *Abutilon vitifolium* and other perennials in soft shades of blue and cream, lead to a hedged enclosure with a sheltered seat. An arched opening in a hedge leads to a bowling green and arbor. Several thatched-roof summerhouses, designed to harmonize with the main house, are placed at axial points along the paths to afford both shelter and architectural interest in the garden.[13] In all, it was a good, solid plan. In 1901, Lady Methuen asked Gertrude Jekyll's advice about turning one area into a rose garden, having disliked Voysey's idea of waves of blue rue. Following a visit to New Place the next spring, Jekyll recommended dwarf rose bushes in each of four beds, with half-standards in the center of each.[14] The gardens at New Place continued to evolve over the years, with the addition of a Japanese garden and water and rock gardens, but Voysey's framework for the grounds has remained undisturbed.

* * *

At first glance, the early architecture of Mackay Hugh Baillie Scott (1865–1945) bears a strong resemblance to that of Voysey, with whitewashed stucco houses, exaggerated gables, and low, swooping rooflines. Like many architects of his generation, Baillie Scott was first exposed to Voysey in *The Studio*. Not as well known or appreciated as Voysey is today, Baillie Scott ran a highly successful practice, specializing in suburban houses with richly decorated interiors. He shared Voysey's disdain for the ugliness of the Victorian era's furnishings, but his interiors were more ornate than Voysey's, with inlay panels and a range of furniture with intricate floral motifs, as well as wallpapers, textiles, metalwork, and stained glass. Blackwell, in Cumbria, one of his grandest houses, is the most complete example of his work today. Designed in 1897 for Edward Holt, a wealthy industrialist, and also located in Cumbria, Blackwell is now a museum. Decorated throughout with furniture, tiles, tex-

Above:
M.H. Baillie Scott, *Blackwell,*
Bowness-on-Windemere, Cumbria.
Courtesy Lakeland Arts Trust,
Cumbria

Below:
M.H. Baillie Scott, *White Lodge*
(Chaplain's House at St. Mary's
Convent), Wantage, Berkshire,
prospective (from *Studio Special*
Number, 1901). Author's Collection

Opposite:
M.H. Baillie Scott, *Heather*
Cottage, perspective (from Baillie
Scott, *Houses and Gardens,* 1906).
Author's Collection

tiles, metalwork, and wood carvings all in floral patterns, it is a fitting tribute to the full capabilities of this pioneer of the Arts and Crafts Movement.[15]

Baillie Scott is a somewhat enigmatic figure, whose appearance resembled "an unassuming countryman," as Betjeman described him, rather than an artist or a businessman.[16] Born in Kent to an affluent family, he was originally slated for life as a farmer in Australia, where his family owned sheep ranches. After studying scientific farming at the Royal Agricultural College, he had a change of heart and decided to become an architect. In the 1880s he was articled to an architect in Bath before moving to the Isle of Man, where he practiced architecture for twelve years. He began experimenting with different styles, particularly Tudor half-timbering, and also came under the influence of the famed Manx silversmith, Archibald Knox, whose distinctive Celtic-inspired style resurfaces in Baillie Scott's interior decorations.

The key to Baillie Scott's successful career lies in his artistic approach to domestic architecture coupled with his affinity for craftsmanship. His early articles for *The Studio,* in which he spelled out the necessity for "simplicity and homely comfort," brought him commissions in England and Europe, including one from Grand Duke Ernest-Ludwig of Hesse to redecorate the Ducal Palace in Darmstadt.[17] In 1901, he also entered the famous House for an Art Lover competition that Mackintosh had entered, winning a coveted prize. Few of his original drawings exist, as his Bedford office was destroyed by

fire in 1919 and the London one suffered bomb damage in 1941. Fortunately his book, *Houses and Gardens*, as well as his articles for *The Studio*, provide a record of his work.

Baillie Scott was more articulate than Voysey and most other Arts and Crafts architects, with the exception of Robert Lorimer, on matters relating to garden design. The opening lines of his 1906 book, *Houses and Gardens*, acknowledges the importance of gardens. "One of the most prominent features in the literature of the last few years has been the garden book, and so numerous have these publications become that every one may learn how a garden should be formed and how maintained," he wrote. "All the gardens described in these books are necessarily attached to houses, and the house as an appendage to the garden meets with a certain degree of attention."[18] This approach was certainly at odds with most architects who viewed the garden as an appendage of the house. By 1933, when he issued the second volume of his work, Baillie Scott's ideas about gardens had matured. "Every architect is necessarily interested in the design of the garden which surrounds the house he has built, just as a painter is interested in the pattern of the frame for the picture he had painted," he wrote. "The garden should, after all, constitute a kind of out-door extension of the building, and may consist of a number of open air apartments connected by corridors which in some cases link themselves with those of the house, so that the house and garden together form a complete arrangement of indoor and outdoor rooms."[19]

Because Baillie Scott designed modestly scaled suburban houses, his ideas were tempered to the homeowner who could not afford elaborate upkeep. "The function of the garden is to grow fruit and vegetables for the household, and also to provide outdoor apartments for the use of the family in fine weather," he stated simply. For a small garden, however, the stiff lines between the kitchen and pleasure gardens needed to be blurred. "The grey-green foliage and great thistle-like heads of the globe artichoke, the mimic forest of the asparagus bed, and the quaint inflorescence of the onion have each a distinctive beauty of their own which would be more widely recognised if these plants were not used for food," he wrote. Some of his ideas, such as the incorporation of a small orchard ("the trees, once planted in grass, will require but little attention") or a woodland copse ("demands absolutely no labour") were somewhat naïve.[20]

For Heather Cottage, one of the houses featured in *Houses and Gardens*, he proposed blending the natural stands of heather with a formal garden near the house. "On sunny hills, where purple heather grows, purple heather shall be the dominant note," he advised.[21] The long, low white house, with a swooping red-tiled roof, sits comfortably in the heath, with hills of heather rising in the background. How different Baillie Scott's perspectives, with their soft, romantic gardens, were from Voysey's more dramatic views, with flowers reduced to decorative elements. A long pergola, which serves to screen the drive from the lawn, provides an important architectural component.

Baillie Scott's recommendations for architectural features, such as a seat or a summerhouse at the end of a vista, a dipping well for watering the garden, dovecotes ("a homely note"), and arbors and pergolas, were always practical. "A garden," he wrote, "should be full of mystery, surprises, and light and shade. One of its most attractive features [is] **the pergola,** with its paved walk checkered by the shadows of the climbing plants which form its walls and roof." Pergolas serve to link the house with the garden as seen in Baillie Scott's rendering of the rose-laden chalk pergola at Undershaw, in Guildford (published in *The Studio* in 1909). The tile-roofed, half-timber and brick cottage with an informal flagged walk has sunken gardens on either side of the pergola, an excellent example of "open-air compartments connected by corridors." The garden is awash with candybox groupings of delphiniums, lilies, lupine, dianthus, and other cottage-garden flowers. Echoing the words of Gertrude Jekyll, whose books Baillie Scott considered an infallible guide to garden planning, he advised massing flowers in informal clumps, planted so that "at each season of the year something is in bloom there, and in blooming forms a well-studied arrangement of colour."[22]

Opposite:
M. H. Baillie Scott, Proposed House (Undershaw) at Guildford, Surrey, perspective (from *The Studio,* May 1909). Author's Collection

Right:
M. H. Baillie Scott, Runton Old Hall, Norfolk, 1998

Unlike Voysey, Baillie Scott was equally at home restoring old manor houses as he was designing new houses, and two excellent examples of his garden planning relate to old manor houses. At Runton Old Hall, Baillie Scott collaborated with Gertrude Jekyll, one of three projects he worked on with her.[23] Jekyll's introduction to Baillie Scott came in 1907 when he wrote to her on behalf of a client. "We are anxious to have some good perennial borders and a good selection of roses for a rose garden and pergola," he wrote. "I have always had such a great appreciation of your books on gardening."[24] The following year, she assisted with the gardens at Runton Old Hall, located near the sea in Norfolk, where the manor house had suffered from recent disfigurements by a ruthless modern builder, according to Baillie Scott.[25] Baillie Scott restored the flint-and-brick house, added a new wing, and planned a garden to complement the house. He devised a series of paved courts set with cobblestones in patterns, brick-and-flint walls to subdivide the garden into spaces and reduce the effect of the seaside winds, and archways for the main vistas. "The final touch to this garden scheme," he wrote, "was added by Miss Jekyll, who arranged the flowers to secure well-thought-out schemes of colour at all seasons." Even though Baillie Scott credited the client, Bertram Hawker, for his artistic sensibilities, Hawker rejected so many of Jekyll's ideas that one plan marked "thrown out" betrays her irritation.[26] Little survives of Jekyll's plantings, but Baillie Scott's thoughtful layout remains intact. The flint-and-brick archways and walls, as well as the patterned stone paths in the courts, provide an exceptional example of how a garden could be designed to relate to the house architecturally.

Snowshill Manor, an old Cotswold manor house in a tiny village near Broadway, in Gloucestershire, reveals Baillie

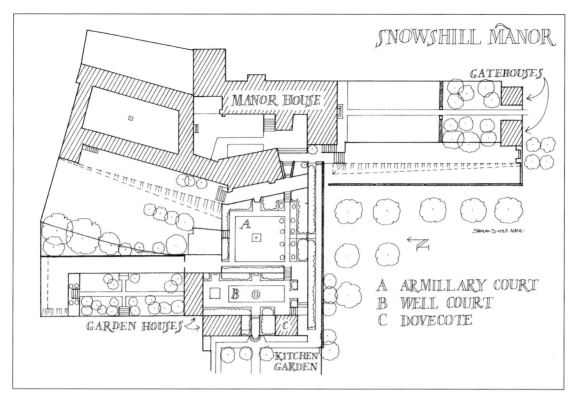

Simon Dorrell, Garden plan for Snowshill Manor, 2003

Opposite: *M. H. Baillie Scott, Snowshill Manor, Snowshill, Gloucestershire, 1986*

Overleaf: *M. H. Baillie Scott, Well Court at Snowshill Manor, 1989*

Scott's ingenuity in garden planning. Dating to 1500, with numerous later additions and dependencies, the manor house was desolate and surrounded by a sea of wilderness in 1919, when architect and antiquarian Charles Paget Wade rescued it, devoting much of his life to restoring the house and amassing a large collection of antiques, artifacts, and whimseys. Wade's winning entry in a competition for a small garden organized by *The Studio* bears a striking resemblance to the arrangement at Snowshill, with a series of courts and long vistas.[27] Until recently it was assumed that Wade had designed those gardens, but plans have surfaced bearing Baillie Scott's name.[28] Most likely, Wade conceived the basic layout and Baillie Scott provided the technical expertise.

What Wade and Baillie Scott did so successfully was to tie together the different levels and outbuildings—the land slopes steeply to the south where the derelict farmyards once stood—into one cohesive unit with informal regularity. From the top terrace, one looks down on the various walled enclosures and across to the fields in the distance; from the

Armillary Court below, one can glimpse the stone manor house through columnar yews. "The design was planned as a series of separate courts, sunny ones contrasting with shady ones and different courts for different moods," Wade wrote. "The plan of the garden is more important than the flowers in it. Mystery is most valuable in garden design; never show all there is at once. Plan for enticing vistas with a hint of something beyond."[29]

The dovecote and farm sheds that Wade had restored were skillfully tied into the plan so that each area retained its individuality, while complementing the others. Changing levels, vistas, and architectural features throughout give the garden its uniqueness. In addition to an armillary sphere, columns, a sundial, an ancient well, and all manner of statuary, Wade further embellished the garden with his favorite color, turquoise, which he thought a good foil for the green grass and foliage. In Wade's day, Snowshill was an architect's garden with little emphasis on flowers, but today it is filled with many beautiful plantings and is a splendid example of Baillie Scott's planning principles.

Chapter 6 | The Art and Craft of Garden-Making.

By the early 1900s, writing about garden design in Britain advanced from the theoretical to the practical. With the publication of two outstanding books, *The Art and Craft of Garden-Making* and *Gardens for Small Country Houses*, garden design became an identifiable entity, rather than an adjunct of architecture. Many books covered the details of horticulture and planting design, but few explained the practicalities of designing and laying out small properties from the homeowner's viewpoint. Sedding, Blomfield, and their followers had enlightened people about the proper attitude regarding garden design, but it fell to Thomas Mawson and Gertrude Jekyll to demonstrate exactly how to execute these ideas.

One of the few designers who was not an architect by training, Thomas Hayton Mawson (1861–1933) successfully bridged the gap between horticulture and architecture. Mawson referred to himself variously as "garden architect," "landscape gardener," and "landscape architect," thus revealing the inexactitude of the profession then in its formative years.[1] Although primarily associated with Cumbria and Yorkshire, in later years Mawson had one of the largest British and international practices of his generation.[2] An exceptionally competent designer, especially in architectural detailing, his work as a whole lacks the passion and individuality of many other garden architects, mainly because he had no identifiable style.

The key to Mawson's success was the combination of his exceptional knowledge of practical horticulture and technical skills. Early in his career, he worked in a family nursery business and attended a technical school, where he learned drawing and drafting, experience that coalesced when he and his brother Robert established Lakeland Nurseries in Windermere in the Lake District. Robert managed the horticultural side of the business and Thomas designed the grounds for their clients. Mawson's first significant client was Colonel Thomas Myles Sandys, who commissioned him to lay out six acres of grounds at Graythwaite Hall in Lancashire in 1889. At Graythwaite, the assignment required extensive earth-moving and grading in order to take advantage of the picturesque quality of the grounds and give definition to the ancestral house. Mawson designed a sweeping drive, stone terraces, and a formal garden filled with yew topiaries as well as specified landscape plantings throughout the property. At Graythwaite he met the architect

Above:
Thomas H. Mawson,
Graythwaite Hall, Ulverston,
Cumbria, 1987

Opposite:
Thomas H. Mawson, Formal
garden at Graythwaite Hall, 1987

Dan Gibson, who subsequently worked for him for two years
before establishing an independent architectural practice.
"He exercised a great influence on the work of the office,"
Mawson recalled, "and set up as high an ideal for the architectural section of our work as I had striven for in landscape
expression."[3] Gibson, whose work was lauded in Gertrude
Jekyll's book, *Garden Ornament*, excelled in the design of
sundials, gates, and garden houses, which added an addi-
tional cachet to Mawson's practice.[4]

Although Mawson's career is heralded today for its international scope, it is his early work as a regional garden designer
that reveals his commitment to the Arts and Crafts Movement.
By 1901, Mawson opened a London office (next door to
Mallows's) in addition to the one in Windermere. Of all
his clients, his greatest was Sir William Lever (later Lord
Leverhulme), who commissioned four significant gardens,
including Mawson's masterpiece, the classically inspired
garden at The Hill, Hampstead, London, with its extraordinary
range of pergolas.[5]

Mawson's greatest legacy is his book, *The Art and Craft of
Garden-Making*, first published with his own funds in 1900.
Literally an overnight success, one reviewer hailed it as a wor-

Thomas H. Mawson, Gardens at Bailrigg, near Lancaster, watercolor by E. A. Chadwick
(from *Studio Yearbook of Decorative Art,* 1908). Author's Collection

Thomas H. Mawson, Little Onn Hall, Stafford, 1989

thy successor to Sedding's book ten years earlier.[6] A second edition appeared the next year, followed by three more; the final edition of 1926, written with his son E. Prentice Mawson, is considered the definitive work on Mawson's career. Today the book is regarded as the first modern work to address the extent of responsibilities entailed in landscape architecture. Dedicated to his first client and mentor, Colonel Sandys, Mawson also acknowledged his indebtedness to Mallows, Griggs, and others who provided illustrations for his book. Later editions include color plates by artists Ernest Albert Chadwick and Ernest Arthur Rowe, whose illustrations regularly appeared in *The Studio*. Between the first and second editions, the book grew by leaps and bounds from a quarto size to a heavy folio of over four hundred pages.

His book clearly made a case for both the *art* and *craft* of garden-making. Written in plain English, with appealing illustrations, it blended theory with practical details of design and planting. It was addressed to potential clients to help them understand the scope of what a garden designer does and provide them with sample solutions, whether an overall plan of the grounds or details of the architectural embellishments and garden furnishings that his firm specialized in. Mawson's book also brought a new dimension to the professional rendering of landscape plans that included topography, elevations, and sight-lines as opposed to romanticized visions of gardens on paper.

On a visit to the Olmsted Brothers in Brookline, Massachusetts, the leading firm of its day, Mawson was impressed by the thoroughness of their approach and their working methods. "In the matter of office organization we in England have much to learn [and] their survey and contour work, which formed the basis of every plan, was done with a thoroughness seldom attempted at home," he wrote. "The method of preparing the plans by regular stages, ending with the work of the men who take out the quantities for trees and shrubs required, all carefully noted on the plans, was a revelation to me."[7] Because Mawson was able to define and illustrate the role of a landscape architect in a way that had not been done before, *The Art and Craft of Garden-Making* was hailed by academic institutions in America, where the landscape architecture profession was just blossoming with the establishment of a program at Harvard University in 1900. As a result, Mawson received speaking engagements at Harvard, Cornell, and Yale universities on landscape architecture.

Foremost among Mawson's theories was the Arts and Crafts dictum of integrated house and garden, or as he expressed it, "garden design in its relation to the house and its architectural character."[8] *The Art and Craft of Garden-Making* attests to the practical ways in which to ensure this essential harmony, illustrated with examples drawn exclusively from his own work. In essence, Mawson regarded garden design as an art, in which the style of the house dictates the configuration of the garden. He held formality at arm's length, however, preferring to enhance the natural character of the landscape rather than forcing the issue. Whenever possible he used local materials and vernacular detailing in his architectural components. His work benefited greatly from his collaboration with architects such as Gibson, Mallows, Baillie Scott, and Voysey.[9]

His responsibilities ranged from laying out new gardens to reconfiguring old ones laid out by other designers. Little Onn Hall, near Stafford, designed for the Ashton sisters around 1900, is an excellent example of Mawson's ability to conceptualize a comprehensive scheme for improvements where earlier gardens were already in place. Designed in collaboration with Gibson, the results must have pleased Mawson, who included the project in each of the editions of his book.

Foremost in his mind was providing the low-lying Tudor-style house with an "architectural support," as he called it.[10] Since the ground was fairly level, he felt the need to introduce some architectural character to the site. His plan shows how he achieved this with an arrangement of terraces for a rose garden and flower borders that linked with an existing kitchen garden and, farther afield, a moat garden. The surrounding grounds were enhanced with plantations of rhododendrons, azaleas, lilacs, yews, and holly trees to complement mature oak, elm, and sycamore trees. To give more architectural form to the terraces, he planted Irish yews clipped into squares and pyramids. As he wrote, "the architectural details have a great influence on the scheme as a whole."[11] The rose garden, opposite the front courtyard, was planted with masses of old-fashioned varieties, such as China roses, damask roses, and the York and Lancaster rose; the enclosure walls were covered in tea and noisette roses. Little Onn Hall combines the best of old and new, as well as a delicate balance between architectural and horticultural elements.

Dyffryn Gardens near Cardiff, South Wales, is probably Mawson's best surviving garden and fully encapsulates his design philosophy.[12] The site, in a sheltered valley, with undulating pasture lands and picturesquely timbered forest trees, was ideal. In 1906, Mawson received the commission from the philanthropist John Cory to extend the existing gardens,

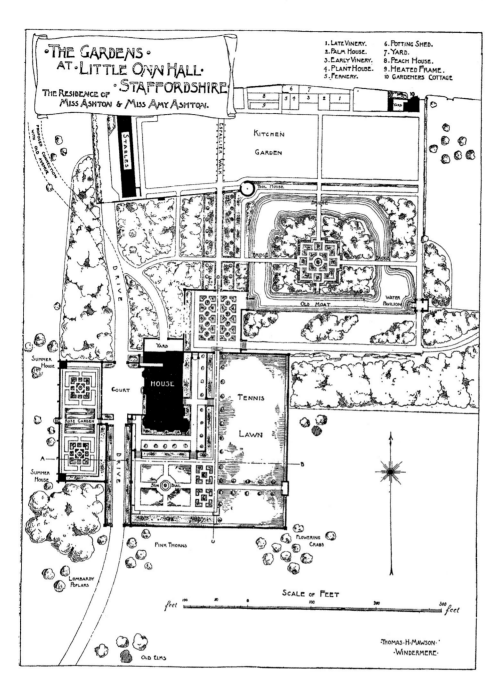

The Gardens at Little Onn Hall · Staffordshire · The Residence of Miss Ashton & Miss Amy Ashton.

1. LATE VINERY.
2. PALM HOUSE.
3. EARLY VINERY.
4. PLANT HOUSE.
5. FERNERY.
6. POTTING SHED.
7. YARD.
8. PEACH HOUSE.
9. HEATED FRAME.
10 GARDENERS COTTAGE

KITCHEN GARDEN

STABLES

ESPALIER WALK

PROPOSED CONNECTION WITH OLD AVENUE

DRIVE

TOOL HOUSE

BRIDGE

BRIDGE

OLD MOAT

WATER PAVILION

SUMMER HOUSE

COURT

HOUSE

YARD

ROSE GARDEN

TENNIS

LAWN

SUMMER HOUSE

A

DRIVE

SUN DIAL

B

U

PINK THORNS

FLOWERING CRABS

LOMBARDY POPLARS

SCALE OF FEET

feet 100   50   0   100   200   300 feet

·THOMAS·H·MAWSON·
·WINDERMERE·

OLD ELMS

Thomas H. Mawson, The Gardens at Little Onn Hall, Staffordshire, the Residence of Miss Ashton and Miss Amy Ashton, *line drawing (from Mawson,* Art and Craft of Garden-Making, *1901).* Author's Collection

Opposite top:
Thomas H. Mawson: Dyffryn Gardens, Cardiff, 2003

Opposite bottom:
Thomas H. Mawson, Plan of Grounds, Duffryn (Dyffryn) Near Cardiff for Reginald Cory, *line drawing (from Mawson,* Art and Craft of Garden-Making, *1926).* Courtesy Marion Pressley

which had been laid out in 1893 when the house was built. After Cory's death four years later, Mawson's extensive plans were implemented by his son, Reginald Cory, a well-known horticulturist and plant collector who proved to be an ideal client.[13] Unusually, Mawson did not include a discussion of the project until the final edition of his book, perhaps to preserve the privacy of his client.

In his plan for the fifty-five-acre property, Mawson added a great lawn to the south front of the sprawling Victorian house to "provide a restful base to the house." To enhance the setting, he added a long axial canal and lily pond extending from the balustrade near the house to the lake in the distance. In contrast to the serenity of the south front, Mawson, encouraged by his client's passion for gardening, created a riot of special gardens—rock gardens, rose gardens, a Pompeiian garden, terraced gardens, pond gardens, herbaceous borders, and "most important of all, the pinetum and experimental gardens"—on the east and west sides. The result, he wrote, was one of "startling contrasts and surprises [and because] each garden is enclosed in its own screen of architecture or foliage, it seldom clashes with its neighbour."[14]

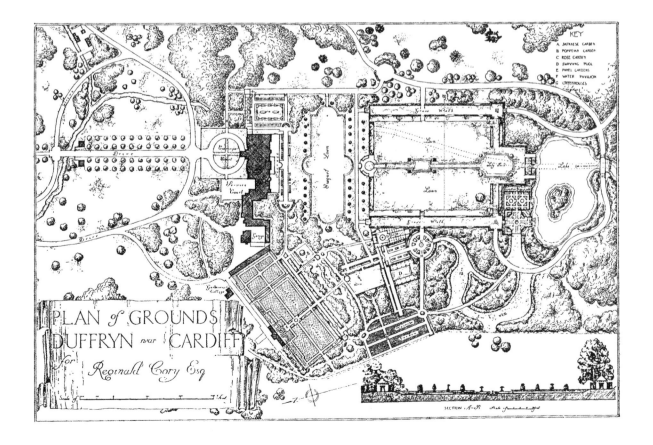

H. Inigo Triggs, Little Boarhunt, Liphook, Hampshire, 1912. Country Life Picture Library

Influential as Mawson's book was, *Gardens for Small Country Houses,* by Gertrude Jekyll and Lawrence Weaver, probably had a greater impact than any book of the era on the practical issues of garden design for the average homeowner. First published in 1912, it served as a companion volume to *Country Life's* popular *Small Country Houses of To-Day* series, which spotlighted recent work by Arts and Crafts architects. The authors noted in the preface to their book that it "filled a place hitherto empty, on the bookshelves of the garden-loving public."[15] Unlike Mawson's, their book was aimed primarily at owners of moderate-sized houses in affluent communities, but it also had a wide appeal among professional garden designers and architects alike, especially in America. For years it was considered the "bible" of formal garden design princi-

ples, and even today, nearly one hundred years after its publication, it is still a major resource for garden designers, landscape architects, and architects.

The Arts and Crafts approach to garden-making, with its emphasis on practicality and ingenuity, unfolds in the pages of *Gardens for Small Country Houses* through schemes by many of the key architects of the day, including Lorimer, Lutyens, Mallows, and Voysey. The heart of the book is the well-honed selection of *Country Life's* incomparable photographs, Jekyll's delightful plans, and the authors' insightful commentary. Like Mawson's book, *Gardens for Small Country Houses* covers similar topics, but it was not nearly as encyclopaedic. Its success lies in its broader focus on both new and historic gardens, rather than on the work of a single designer.

Unlike earlier manifestos by Blomfield and others, *Gardens for Small Country Houses* is a far cry from pompous historicism and rigid rules. The advice offered is always inspirational, yet practical. "Our noble English yew is nearly always beneficial in the garden landscape," the authors wrote. "Whether as a trimmed hedge or as a fast-growing tree, its splendid richness of deepest green, and, indeed, its whole aspect is of the utmost value."[16] The prose may be somewhat flowery, but the advice is always solid, without a shred of romanticism.

What also distinguishes the book is its expert selection of gardens suited to various small sites. Examples of the work of Lutyens and Jekyll abound (see Chapter 8), but others, such H. Inigo Triggs's own garden, **Little Boarhunt,** in Liphook, are equally skillful in their planning. They included it as an example of "how the qualities that make the beauty of the historic formal gardens may be reproduced . . . for houses of moderate size." Whether King John actually ran a boar through the grounds is a matter of dispute, but Triggs captured some of the romance of a bygone era in his well-considered scheme for a sunken parterre in the former farmyard. The enclosure nestles into the L-shaped house, with the other two sides framed by brick pergolas and a garden house in one corner, "inexpensively built a single brick thick, with its faces cemented." A long water rill runs the length of the enclosure, with a central rectangular pool that serves for watering the garden. A figure of a boy with a fish rises from a slender brick column in the center of the pool, and a brick dovecote anchors the north wall. "The sunk garden itself is an admirable example of the wealth of interesting detail that can be employed in a small space without creating any feeling of overcrowding."[17] Thanks to their exposure in *Gardens for Small Country Houses*, the water rill, garden house, and dovecote at Little Boarhunt soon became much-imitated features in British and American gardens, just as the work of Lutyens and Jekyll held wide appeal among landscape architects worldwide. Hand in hand with a layout that worked so naturally with the house, Arts and Crafts gardens were renowned for their detailing, which both books explain. Steps, paving, summerhouses, pergolas, trelliswork, garden furnishings, and water features all fell into this category. Mawson concurred with Jekyll and Weaver, that "nothing imparts character to a garden, and gives more interest, than well designed and carefully executed architectural details."[18] The stone steps and paving that seem so technically correct in Mawson's work burst into life in *Gardens for Small Country Houses*, especially in Lutyens's designs, where the paving has just the right amount of irregularity and his signature half-moon steps provide a pleasing method of connecting changes in levels. "Although stairways are among the most useful elements in garden design, and give just opportunity for conscious architectural treatment" wrote Jekyll and Weaver, "it is not always desirable to force the note of formality."[19]

One of the most ancient ways of defining outdoor spaces is through the use of hedges, or living greenery. They serve as a background for flower borders, a neat enclosure for a bowling green, or an ornamental device to be clipped and pruned into decorative shapes; they offer architectural interest. Used by nearly every Arts and Crafts architect, hedges not only provided drama in perspective renderings, but also worked well on the ground. Mawson recommended yew and holly hedges to enhance the effect of flowers against their dark background, but advocated simpler forms of clipped hedges. "The simpler forms . . . are the most satisfactory because they express their purpose without any show or pretense, [but] it is well to avoid heads clipped to the forms of wild beasts, peacocks, etc., unless to express some symbolic meaning."[20]

Enclosure walls of brick or stone not only ensure privacy and shelter, but can extend the parameters of the house. Arched openings allow easy access from one area to the next. If these are covered with vines, care should be taken not to smother the walls and obliterate their beauty, one of Jekyll's pet peeves. Low retaining walls, typically in rough stone of the region, can be enhanced with careful plantings of alpines in the wall joints and a judicious selection of small shrubs and rambling roses at the foot. Jekyll thought that such low walls were enhanced by plantings on the top, rather than at the foot.

Formal water features, such as long canals, waterlily ponds, reflecting pools, or small fountains, add immeasurably to small gardens. Mawson even questioned whether a garden was complete without water, whether a small reflecting pool or an architecturally treated pond with fountains and cascades derived from the great European gardens. Jekyll and Weaver recommended that the water, whether set in turf or in a paved

court, "should be kept at its proper level, which is as high as possible. The nearer it is to the kerb of the pool, the wider and more beautiful will be the reflections."[21]

Arbors and pergolas also lent charm to a garden. Constructed of brick piers, rough stone, or masonry, and covered with climbing roses, wisteria, or fragrant vines, they afforded a shady retreat in the hot weather. They could be embellished with chains linking the posts for growing swags of roses. Lutyens, who used pergolas to great effect for reinforcing the geometry of the garden, often had alternating round and square piers for visual interest. Pergolas were versatile because when densely planted they could enclose the garden entirely, but when sparsely planted or discontinuous they drew the eye to the greater landscape in the distance. In kitchen gardens, rustic pergolas constructed of larch poles, were perfect for growing gourds.

One of the most important elements of gardens of the Arts and Crafts era were the small buildings, such as informal gazebos, thatched pavilions, stone summerhouses, or whimsical dovecotes. Their success, wrote Jekyll and Weaver, "depends as much upon their skilful placing as upon their form and materials." The building was usually integrated into the scheme either at the end of a long walk or at the corner of a garden wall, but the most important aspect was that its style should reflect the architecture of the main house and be built of local materials.

A well-placed garden bench, either a stone one built into the wall with plenty of paving in front of it or a wooden one of special design, adds to the enjoyment of the garden. "Good design in garden furniture is just as necessary to the success of a garden as the furniture to the house itself," advised Mawson.[22] Lutyens's signature bench, which made its first appearance at Munstead Wood in the late 1890s and proliferates in the pages of catalogues today, has somewhat overshadowed thoughtfully designed ones by his fellow architects. Mawson thought that oak was the best choice because it lasted the longest, but for a painted one, "nothing looks so well as green painted pine."[23] Jekyll thought the best was untreated oak that eventually takes on silvery hues, and also observed that regularly painted ones stood up well too. As to the appropriate color, however, green is doubtful "as it is likely to quarrel with the varied natural greens which are near it [and] white is safe, but looks rather staring during the seasons when there is no brilliant colour in the flower garden to relieve it."[24] Mawson, Jekyll, and Weaver had their points of dispute about what was best and how to achieve it, but in the end their recommendations have proved timeless.

Edwin Lutyens, Pergola at Hestercombe, 1990

Chapter 7 | At Home with Two Master Gardeners.

Gardens of the Arts and Craft era might have been little more than a curious historical episode had it not been for William Robinson (1838–1935) and Gertrude Jekyll (1843–1932). Near contemporaries, their careers ran along parallel lines. Each possessed an exceptional horticultural knowledge and wrote more than a dozen important books, but their backgrounds and personalities were entirely different. Born in Ireland of dubious parentage, Robinson was a shrewd businessman, while Jekyll, who was born in the more genteel environment of London's Mayfair, was an artist at heart. Like Morris's Red House, their own homes expressed their individuality and the fruits of their labors. Robinson's Gravetye Manor was Elizabethan in origin and surrounded by 1,000 acres of bucolic fields and woodlands, while Jekyll's Munstead Wood was a more modest affair, fifteen acres of grounds enveloping a modern cottage designed by Edwin Lutyens.

William Robinson was considered the prophet of wild gardening and an unswerving advocate for the cultivation of hardy plants at a time when bedding-out with tender annuals was the accepted practice in British gardens. Jekyll's reputation rests equally on her writings and her practical work as a garden designer, while Robinson's legacy lies primarily in the incomparable array of publications he either wrote or edited.[1] His two most important books—*The Wild Garden* (1870) and *The English Flower Garden* (1883)—were perennial favorites among many generations of gardeners and the various magazines that he edited held a wide appeal to amateur and professional gardeners alike.[2]

The Wild Garden, which cautioned that unmanaged wilderness was not the same as landscapes enhanced by carefree perennials, opened many readers' eyes to the natural beauty of indigenous plants. Jekyll consulted *The Wild Garden* when she developed her gardens at Munstead Wood in the 1880s and 1890s and many Americans acknowledged their indebtedness to the book in their landscape planning. Wilhelm Miller, an influential American editor and horticultural writer, formulated a style of landscape design suited to the Midwest based directly on Robinson's books. *The English Flower Garden*, compiled mainly from articles published in *The Garden*, a journal that Robinson edited for decades, was one of the first modern-day compilations of cultural information and design advice aimed at home gardeners. Sprinkled with line drawings by artists and pithy commentary on design matters, it was an immensely popular book. There were fifteen editions in Robinson's lifetime and it has been continuously in print since its initial publication in 1883.[3] When Miller visited Gravetye after reading both these books, he gasped at the "luxurious abandon" of its plantings and the "glorious scale" with which wild gardening was being carried out.[4]

In comparison with Jekyll's worldwide renown today, Robinson's reputation suffers somewhat by comparison due to his dogmatic personality. Despite the fact that his publications were revolutionary in their day, they lack the elegant writing style that sets Jekyll's books apart and consequently are appreciated primarily by specialists. Robinson, however, was a master of marketing his knowledge through books and journals. More cosmopolitan than Jekyll, he visited Europe and the United States, where he met the leading botanists, horticulturists, and designers of the day. In 1870, for instance, his visit to Central Park and Mount Auburn Cemetery (known for its splendid trees and ornamental shrubs) fanned his interest in public gardens, while Horatio Hollis Hunnewell's famed pinetum near Boston left him in awe of American gardeners.

In the 1880s, when Gertrude Jekyll was just beginning to write gardening pieces for *The Garden*, Robinson was firmly established in the field. After the publication of her first book, *Wood and Garden*, in 1899, it quickly became apparent that Jekyll's talents went far beyond mere horticultural knowledge. To her books and to the hundreds of gardens she designed Jekyll brought the full panoply of her multiple skills as artist, craftswoman, antiquarian, architectural connoisseur, and horticulturist. *The Studio* noted that she had "the trained eye of an artist as well as the eloquent pen of the ready writer," something that could not have been said of Robinson, who was basically a reporter.[5] By the time *Colour in the Flower Garden* was published in 1908, both the author and her garden at Munstead Wood were world famous, whereas Gravetye Manor was known only to Robinson's inner circle of friends.

In 1885, when he bought Gravetye Manor in Sussex, Robinson had already written ten books and founded at least five periodicals, of which *The Garden* and *Gardening Illustrated* were the most successful. Orginally built in 1598, Gravetye Manor is ideally situated in the rolling countryside of the Weald of Sussex, with easy access by rail to Robinson's editorial offices in London. The large stone manor house stands midway on a hill, the north side protected from the winds and the south front overlooking the expansive view. Over the years he transformed both house and garden, publishing a detailed record of his yearly progress in *Gravetye Manor, or Twenty Years' Work Round an Old Manor House*.[6] For the interior renovations and additions to the manor house, he turned to George Devey, whose work there greatly displeased Robinson.[7] He then engaged Ernest George of the London architectural firm George and Peto, whose most famous pupil was Edwin Lutyens. Lutyens, who later designed a boathouse on one of the lakes at Gravetye, found Robinson exasperating, boring, and full of contradictions. Jesting with Blomfield one day, Lutyens suggested "cutting a statue of W. Robinson in yew! as a monument to all he has done for gardening."[8]

Referring to the still-simmering controversies initiated by Sedding and Blomfield, Robinson snapped in one of his regular columns for *Country Life*, "There is so much phrasemongering in matters of garden design and art that it is better to deal with actual work."[9] Gravetye's garden and landscape entailed a tremendous amount of work, including massive earth-moving and the building of walls, terraces, and pergolas. In addition to the garden and pleasure grounds, there were hundreds of acres of fields, meadows, and naturalistically planted woodlands. The pleasure grounds were initially conceived along gardenesque lines, but Robinson several years later changed the naturally sloping grade near the house to flat stone terraces that exemplified Blomfield's stance, which Robinson had vehemently rejected not long before. Unlike Blomfield, however, Robinson dealt with the greater landscape beyond the immediate house. He wrote, "There is no reason why the garden, which in our country is so often the foreground to a beautiful landscape, should not itself be a picture always."[10]

Initially the flower gardens consisted of simple beds close to the house filled with tufted pansies, self-colored carnations, and roses, with the emphasis on the plants themselves rather than on the design of the borders.

Overleaf:
Gravetye Manor, East Grinstead, West Sussex, 1988

Opposite:
Beatrice Parsons (1870–1955),
Spring Woods, Gravetye, Sussex,
watercolor. Mallett and Son
Antiques, London

"I am a flower gardener," he wrote, "and not a mere spreader-about of bad carpets done in reluctant flowers." A garden should contain "the greatest number of favourite plants in the simplest way." With that in mind, he "threw the ground into simple beds, suiting the space for convenience of working and planting, not losing an inch more than was necessary for walks."[11] Henry James left a memorable record of Gravetye's gardens when he wrote, "Few things in England can show a greater wealth of bloom than the wide flowery terrace immediately beneath the gray, gabled house, where tens of thousands of tea-roses . . . divide their province with the carnations and pansies [and] the medley of tall yuccas and saxifrage."[12]

As Robinson was fine-tuning his flower gardens, he was assiduously buying up neighboring farms and woods until he had amassed nearly 1,000 acres. His great love was Gravetye's carefully managed woodlands, planted with native plants, including sweeps of thousands of **daffodils.**

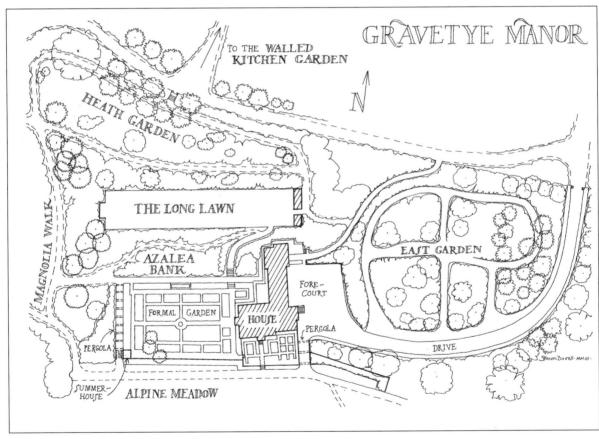

Home Landscapes, a companion volume to *Gravetye Manor*, eulogizes his woodlands. The rolling terrain of his estate soon resembled the naturalistic beauties of an eighteenth-century picturesque landscape, replete with a herd of pedigree Sussex cattle whose deep red color provided a perfect foil for the green countryside.

As his passion for plants consumed him, Robinson's collection of flowers, fruits, shrubs, and trees (some of which came from America) grew to substantial proportions. His water gardens, for instance, included one of the largest collections of waterlilies in Europe, including a special tank devoted to rare specimens acquired from the French breeder Latour-Marliac. Pergolas were festooned with hundreds of varieties of his world-famous clematises. His walled kitchen garden, built in 1896, housed an unsurpassed collection of vegetables and fruits, some of which were espaliered on the walls. He paved the small garden flanking the south porch with old flagstones from London, filling the beds with plants in shades of lilac, purple, pink, and silver. On higher ground, near the north face of the manor house, he developed an azalea bank and, higher still, a garden devoted exclusively to heathers, separated by a traditional bowling green. On the south side of the manor house, a large alpine meadow was planted with masses of naturalized scillas, daffodils, anemones, and fritillarias. The east garden, off the entry court, was devoted to magnolias and other ornamental trees and shrubs, including a rare specimen, *Davidia involucrata* (Dove Tree), first introduced from China in 1904.

For many, the most breathtaking part of Gravetye was the west paved garden, brimming with tea and China roses and surrounded by pergolas, arbors, and trellises. In its heyday the garden was given over to nearly thirty beds of roses and their companion plants, such as dianthus, violas, pansies, forget-me-nots, and carnations whose colors were chosen to complement the gray stone manor house. In the northwest corner stands a stone summerhouse designed in 1900 by Ernest George, who also designed the pedestal for the central sundial, placed at the crossing of the two main paths paved with old stones from London rather than high-maintenance gravel. In later years, when Robinson was confined to a wheelchair, some of the paths were remade as stone ramps.

Robinson considered the west and south flower gardens, which open out directly from doors in the house, as "a larger living-room" and "in intimate relation to the house," the stance taken by the formalists in the 1890s. "The real flower garden, where all our precious flowers are," he commented, should be "in close relation to the house, so that we can enjoy and see and gather our flowers in the most direct way. . . . Going for a half a mile to get to the flower garden, as happens in some Scotch places, or scattering garden flowers in all directions, is not the right way," he concluded.[13]

In the belief that his gardens were "full of pictures," Robinson invited many noted landscape painters to paint them. "I have worked long and hard to prove that the garden, instead of being a horror to the artist, may be the very heart of his work," he commented.[14] Among his favored artists were Henry G. Moon, a botanical illustrator for *The Garden* who was renowned for his exacting depictions of flowers and his sensitive Corot-inspired landscape paintings, and Alfred Parsons, who illustrated many of Robinson's publications and was a garden designer of some note. Moon's drawings, which were simply executed and full of life and character, appealed to Robinson the most. His landscape paintings of Gravetye's woodlands still hang in Gravetye Manor today.[15]

At Robinson's death in 1935, Gravetye was left to the Forestry Commission, with the stipulation that there be no lectures or technical instruction because "the trees, woods, and landscape shall be the only teachers."[16] After lying derelict for years, the manor house and thirty acres were leased in 1958 to restaurateur Peter Herbert, who proceeded to transform Robinson's home into one of the leading country house hotels in Britain. The initial clearing of the garden took over two years.[17] All the main garden areas have been completely refurbished and the once-dense central flower beds in the west garden have been replaced by a smooth green lawn. Today Gravetye is a monument to William Robinson's ideals. As he said when he launched *Flora and Sylva* (a short-lived luxury journal with color plates by Henry Moon), "I married Flora to Sylva, a pair not far apart in Nature, only in books." The same could be said of Gravetye.

Opposite top:
Alfred Parsons (1847–1920), *South Terrace, Gravetye Manor.* Gravetye Manor Collection, courtesy Peter Herbert

Opposite bottom:
Simon Dorrell, Garden plan for Gravetye Manor, 2003

Top:
Beatrice Parsons (1870–1955),
West Paved Garden, watercolor.
Christopher Wood Gallery,
London

Above:
Beatrice Parsons (1870–1955),
West Paved Garden, watercolor.
Gravetye Manor Collection,
courtesy Peter Herbert

Above:
*Sir Ernest George's summer-
house in West Garden, Gravetye
Manor, 1994*

Munstead Wood, Gertrude Jekyll's home in Surrey, can be considered the perfect expression of the symbiotic nature of house and garden. It became a legend during her lifetime through the many books and articles she wrote about it as well as through personal visits paid by admirers from around the world. Few houses better express their owner's character than Munstead Wood, due to the happy combination of a skilled architect and a determined client. The gardens did not follow a prescribed plan, but evolved over time, and were nearly fully developed before the house was built. When Robert Lorimer visited Munstead Wood in 1897, just six days after Jekyll moved into her new home, he commented that she had laid out all the gardens first and "left a hole in the centre of the ground for the house."[18] It was her architect Edwin Lutyens's ingenious design that inextricably married the house with the garden.

Left:
Gertrude Jekyll's shrub borders at Munstead Wood, 1907 (from Jekyll, *Colour in the Flower Garden,* 1908). Author's Collection

Opposite:
Simon Dorrell, Garden plan for Munstead Wood, 2003

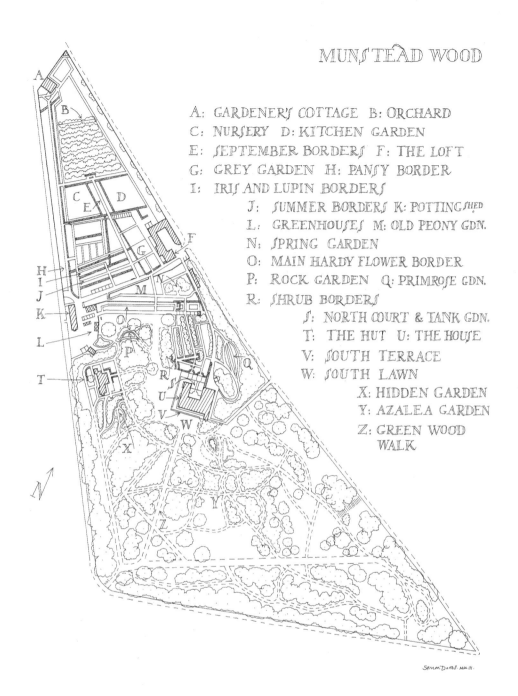

MUNSTEAD WOOD

A: GARDENER'S COTTAGE B: ORCHARD
C: NURSERY D: KITCHEN GARDEN
E: SEPTEMBER BORDERS F: THE LOFT
G: GREY GARDEN H: PANSY BORDER
I: IRIS AND LUPIN BORDERS
J: SUMMER BORDERS K: POTTING SHED
L: GREENHOUSES M: OLD PEONY GDN.
N: SPRING GARDEN
O: MAIN HARDY FLOWER BORDER
P: ROCK GARDEN Q: PRIMROSE GDN.
R: SHRUB BORDERS
S: NORTH COURT & TANK GDN.
T: THE HUT U: THE HOUSE
V: SOUTH TERRACE
W: SOUTH LAWN
X: HIDDEN GARDEN
Y: AZALEA GARDEN
Z: GREEN WOOD
WALK

SIMON DORRELL MM III.

Prior to moving to Munstead Wood, Jekyll had lived nearby with her family at Munstead House, where her knowledge of horticulture and unique approach to planting design quickened. The lessons she learned there paid off at Munstead Wood.[19] Robinson, whom she had first met in 1875, visited in 1880 to confer about her garden and perhaps advise on how to lay it out. Two years later *The Garden* published an article about her garden, praising the long border: "Never before have we seen hardy plants set out so well or cultivated in such a systematic way."[20]

Jekyll began gardening at Munstead House in 1878, while she was studying various arts and crafts, but by 1883 she had clearly run out of space. That year she was able to acquire fifteen acres nearby, mostly of "the poorest possible soil."[21] Nonetheless, she used what natural advantages she found there, developing the former Scots pine plantation into woodland gardens and the poor field into her working gardens, reserving the central chestnut copse for the site of her house, which was not built until 1897. In the woodland gardens, Jekyll followed Robinson's suggestions, underplanting areas with

Ghent azaleas at Munstead Wood, 2003

Opposite:
Munstead Wood from the woodland, 2003

masses of rhododendrons or azaleas, giving each path a specific interest, whether ferns and bracken or lilies, to complement the selected groupings of birches, chestnuts, or oaks. She planted rivers of daffodils along ancient pack-horse tracks and established an area devoted to native heaths. Where the lawn met the woods, she planted clumps of lilies, ferns, asters, and other shrubbery-edge plantings, an idea gleaned from Robinson.

As she fully explained and illustrated in *Colour in the Flower Garden*, Jekyll established a number of ornamental gardens devoted to flowers of one season. These included a spring garden, a naturalistic primrose garden, a June cottage garden, and September borders of perennial asters, among others. Her October Michaelmas daisy borders, arranged with mounds of soft blue and purples, provided a "garden picture" in cool months that was not far from the house. Perhaps her most widely acclaimed creation was the main flower border, two hundred feet long and fourteen feet deep, backed by a

high sandstone wall that separated it from the spring garden. The border had a complex and intricate color scheme based on harmonious color relationships, inspired perhaps by one of J.M.W. Turner's paintings. The large central portion had fiery reds fading to orange and deep yellow. The colors continued to fade to paler yellow and pink, culminating at both ends with blues and lilacs in a ground of gray foliage. The whole arrangement was actually an elaborate piece of *trompe-l'oeil*. In order to reach the border, one strolled down a shaded nut walk from the house and through a pergola, emerging into bright sunlight to face a carefully arranged river of color and texture. The whole picture was clearly seen from the lawn, "the cool colouring at the ends [enhancing] the brilliant warmth of the middle and [each section] a picture in itself."[22]

Two acres of Munstead Wood were given over to working gardens, including a kitchen garden, nursery, and a large orchard, which visitors rarely saw. There were numerous cottage-style borders and hedged compartments filled with drifts

Left:
Helen Allingham (1848–1926), *Michaelmas Daisies* (October borders at Munstead Wood), watercolor, c. 1900. Author's Collection

Below left:
Thomas Hunn (1857–1928), *The Pansy Garden, Munstead Wood, Surrey,* watercolor, c. 1900. Mallett and Son Antiques, London

Opposite:
Helen Allingham (1848–1926), *In Munstead Wood Garden* (main flower border), watercolor, c. 1900. Christopher Wood Gallery, London

of China roses, irises, hollyhocks, and her own strain of lupines in special colorations that complemented the gray clapboard barn.[23] Jekyll's large nursery supplied plants for her garden design commissions, while the kitchen garden kept the house supplied with fruits and vegetables. Next to the potting shed and greenhouses, Jekyll had a special garden devoted to pansies. In the garden yard she raised lily-of-the-valley and narcissus, which were sold at Covent Garden. Reserve gardens not only filled the house with flowers, but provided valuable seeds that Jekyll sold to commercial nurseries in England and France.

In Edwin Lutyens (1869–1944), Jekyll found an architect who shared her vernacular sensibilities for home-building and could create a house worthy of her gardens. Lutyens hailed from a small village not far from Munstead. After studying at the South Kensington School of Art (where Jekyll had studied years earlier) and working briefly in the office of Ernest George, he had just set himself up as an architect when he met Gertrude Jekyll in 1889. They liked one another immediately, and soon were scouring the countryside, under Jekyll's direction, looking at old cottages and studying traditional building methods, which they avidly discussed and debated. Jekyll's influence on the young architect is legend; when she asked him to design her house in 1892, they embarked on a fruitful collaboration that resulted in dozens of houses and gardens.

Jekyll's love of simple materials and excellence in craftsmanship extended to the planning and building of all aspects of Munstead Wood, not only the house. One colleague extolled her "passion for matters concerning domestic architecture that almost equals [her] interest in plants and trees."[24] This love of local customs, artifacts, and buildings was recorded in minute detail in her book, *Old West Surrey* (1904). Before settling on a design for the house, Lutyens built two small cottages on the site, one for Jekyll's head gar-dener and the Hut, where she lived for two years while her main house was under construction. Guided by the main requirements for her house, "serenity of mind" and "the feeling of a convent," the resulting design in 1896 brought together everything that she desired. Built of local bargate stone and timber felled on her own property, it "does not stare with newness," as Jekyll commented in *Home and Garden*, nor was it a copy of an old building.[25] Lutyens married a small Tudor-style manor house with a highly personal interpretation of local vernacular style. The house was at once quirky and contrived, but simple, elegant, and eminently comfortable.

Jekyll's study of numerous crafts and appreciation for local customs influenced the furnishing of her house as well as its craftsmanship. The house was steeped in the regional Surrey vocabulary, with half-timbering, deeply hipped roofs, and plain plastered walls. Like those of Morris's Red House, the corridors are timber-lined, with whitewashed walls and oak doors. The furnishings were simple Jacobean chests and tables, and the decorations and ornamentations were mostly Jekyll's own handiwork. In the end, Munstead Wood may have been a large house for a single woman, but it was unpretentious and eminently suited to her.[26]

The character of Munstead Wood was lost after Jekyll's death in 1932, but her many books, articles, and photographs serve to keep its significance alive today. When it went out of family hands in 1948, Munstead Wood was broken up into several parcels. Both the Hut and the gardener's cottage survive, and sections of the original working gardens are now being restored. The house, principal gardens, and woodlands have been in sympathetic hands for the last thirty years. These gardens were rehabilitated in the 1990s, based on a vast store of visual and written information available about the site. Jekyll's shrubbery borders, main flower border, spring garden, and seasonal color borders bloom once again.

The September garden at Munstead Wood, with half-timbered gardener's cottage in distance, 1907 (from Jekyll, *Colour in the Flower Garden,* 1908). Author's Collection

Chapter 8 | A Perfect House and Garden.

The compatibility of the ideas of Edwin Lutyens with those of Gertrude Jekyll led to a fruitful partnership that resulted in some of the most renowned gardens of the early twentieth century. Having a Lutyens house and a Jekyll garden was the ultimate emblem for Britain's new wealthy elite. Even though Jekyll designed hundreds of gardens in her lifetime, those designed with Lutyens best encapsulate the Arts and Crafts approach to garden-making. While Jekyll's planting style remained static—in the 1920s she continued to rely on the formulas she had developed in the 1890s—Lutyens's meteoric career quickly advanced from the Surrey Vernacular style of Munstead Wood to High Georgian in a matter of years. Despite the range of architectural styles represented in his country houses, his gardens associated with Jekyll are firmly entrenched in Arts and Crafts methodology.

Deanery Garden, in Sonning, Berkshire, is one of the best examples of Arts and Crafts methodology. Designed in 1899 for Edward Hudson, founder and managing director of *Country Life*, the magazine that made an undisputed impact on the country house set, it set the standard for the intimacy of house and garden. Jekyll, who wrote gardening notes for *Country Life*, is thought to have introduced Lutyens to Hudson, a rather shy and inarticulate man who had much in common with Lutyens. Both men expressed themselves in their passions rather than in words: Lutyens in buildings and Hudson in his appreciation of country houses that his publications made famous.[1] They enjoyed a lifelong friendship, with Hudson commissioning four projects from Lutyens and publishing accounts of all Lutyens's principal buildings in *Country Life*.[2]

Lutyens's biographer Christopher Hussey called Deanery Garden "a perfect architectural sonnet, compounded of brick and tile and timber forms, in which [Lutyens's] handling of the masses and spaces serve as rhythm: its theme, a romantic bachelor's idyllic afternoons beside a Thames backwater."[3] Hudson's busy schedule led him to sell Deanery Garden a few years after its completion. The starting point for Deanery Garden were the vestiges of the old site, once the house of the Dean of Salisbury. Old brick walls running between the river and the village defined the property outlines and an aging apple orchard provided the romantic setting. Lutyens designed a brick house tight against the wall behind the busy village street, with the principal entrance through a

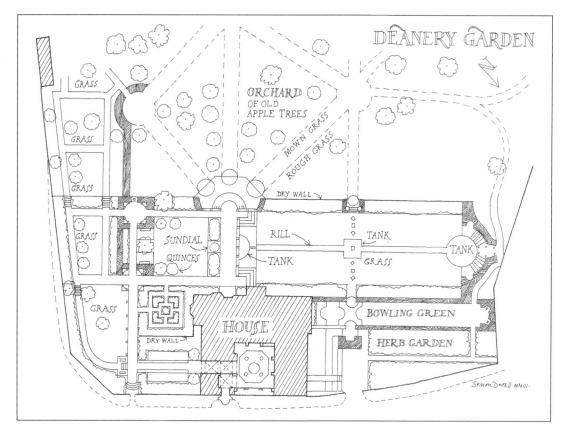

Simon Dorrell, *Garden plan for Deanery Garden,* 2003

door in the wall into a chalk-vaulted cloisterlike passageway (perhaps a nod to the site's ecclesiastical origins) that leads to a formal courtyard enclosed on three sides. Another doorway in the wall opens onto a path with a vine-covered pergola leading to the garden, a trick Jekyll used to great effect at Munstead Wood. Lutyens reused the idea for entrances in a high wall at Millmead.

The gardens are a series of enclosures hugging the house on different levels, each with vistas to the distant orchard. "House and garden are a single interpenetrating conception," wrote Hussey. In his opinion, the design and execution of Deanery Garden, with "Jekyll's naturalistic planting wedded |[to] Lutyens's geometry," settled the steaming controversy between Blomfield and Robinson of formal versus naturalistic garden design.[4] While Hussey's comments, written in 1950, give equal credit to Jekyll, an anonymous *Country Life* article of 1903 omits any reference to her: "Mr. Lutyens never designed a more perfect house or a more charming garden."[5] In *Houses and Gardens of E. L. Lutyens*, Weaver acknowledged Jekyll's work with Lutyens in "producing effects of singular richness."[6]

Deanery Garden has many of Lutyens's trademark features, such as his signature radiating halfmoon steps, linear water rills, semicircular pools, spouting masques, and pergolas with alternating round and square piers, that appear in later gardens. One of the focal points, and the most imitated by other designers, is the long rill, with circular pools (referred to as "tanks" by Jekyll) at both ends and a square pool in the center of the rill. Here Lutyens's fascination with geometry is at its most playful: a path with square stepping stones arranged at alternating angles on the lawn bisects the central square pool; one circular pool is elevated, while the other one is recessed under a bridge-walkway that leads from the house to the orchard; square steps alternate with round ones, and so on. The rill is flanked by wide grass panels with pale-toned flower borders; closer to the house a bowling green runs parallel to the rill garden. The formality of these upper gardens and others near the house fades into the natural element, the orchard.

Deanery Garden was designed for roses, one of Hudson's hobbies. Rose 'The Garland' rambles in the old apple trees and spills out from the tops of the retaining walls throughout

Fenja Gunn, The Deanery Garden, Sonning-on-Thames, Berkshire, watercolor, 1993. Courtesy Fenja Gunn

the garden. These walls have been planted with dianthus, stonecrops, and other wall-loving plants described in Jekyll's book *Wall and Water Gardens*. "The garden is rich in delightful detail," whether the flower borders or the ornamental figures in bronze and stone. It is a "remarkably beautiful and charming garden," wrote Jekyll and Weaver.[7] Deanery Garden provides a perfect balance of old elements with the new; it also balances the architectural detailing found in the pavers and hedging with the informality of the plantings. Deanery Garden, with its various compartmentalized "rooms," is an exceptional example of how to achieve a harmony between house and garden as well as the marriage of formality with informality.

Goddards, along with Orchards and Munstead Wood, is one of Lutyens's most important and original early houses. Located in Abinger Common, Surrey, Goddards is a homespun version of some of his grander confections. The fanciful house, built entirely from local stone and oak with light-colored roughcast walls, jaunty red brick mullions and window surrounds, and a tile roof, provided a perfect setting for a small, enclosed garden court designed by Jekyll. Originally designed in 1898 as a holiday home for working women from the East End of London, it was enlarged and converted to a year-round country house in 1910 for Frederick Mirrielees, the owner. With its twin gables, tall brick chimneys, and distinctive detailing, it is still an unusually well-preserved house.[8] Goddards is also one of the first examples of what would become one of Jekyll's most consistent planting themes, a quiet, welcoming front entrance contrasted with the principal garden in the back, hidden from view of the street.

The focal point of the garden court, nestled between the two splayed wings of the house, is the stone well, around which are grouped low-growing plants "like sea anemones lying on a rock," noted Weaver.[9] This garden court undoubtedly took its inspiration from the north court at Munstead Wood, designed only two years earlier, which is paved, with millstones in the pavement adding a decorative element. The paving, with pockets in the irregular flagstones for sun-loving plants with gray and silver foliage, identifies its function as a terrace rather than as a traditional flower-filled pleasure gar-

Above:
Edwin Lutyens, *Garden front
at Goddards, Surrey,* 1992

Opposite:
Edwin Lutyens, *Goddards, Surrey,*
1899. Country Life Picture Library

den. In her choice of plantings, Jekyll may have considered the institutional or low-maintenance nature of the garden, since the house was originally for summer use only. A low stone wall encircles the well and another marks the outer parameters of the terrace. The linear theme is extended with low, clipped yew hedges that define the outer limits of the garden.

Marsh Court, designed in 1901 for Herbert Johnson, is a far grander and more whimsical house than Goddards, with an architectural garden that looks impressive in photographs, but in reality may not have been too welcoming for actual use. Located in Hampshire, overlooking the River Test, Marsh Court is built from brilliant white chalk with sharply contrasting red brick chimneys and irregular patches of red tiles and black flint decorating the walls. The checkerboard theme is carried out in the terrace paving, in the jagged paved paths, and in the sundial, which matches the exterior of the house. The last of Lutyens's houses modeled after a Tudor manor house, Marsh Court was "Lutyens in his gayest mood," wrote Weaver.[10]

The sunken pool garden is the focal point of the scheme. From the elevated point of the water garden (below which lies a pergola), one can gaze back at the architectural fantasy of the house. Laid out as a "room," the garden functions as an "arm" of the H-shaped house. A long rectangular pool, surrounded by high balustraded walls, is sunk into the multiple folds of low, broad steps. As in some of Lutyens and Jekyll's subsequent work, the paths and landings for the steps are

Edwin Lutyens, *Marsh Court, Hampshire,* 1985

Water garden at Marsh Court, 1985

constructed from York pavers with panels of herringbone-patterned brickwork. Bisecting the pool, a tiny water rill runs from lead cisterns in one high wall to the other. Stone planters are embellished with seahorses spouting water from their muzzles and lead tortoises are arranged along the edges of the pool. These sculptures were made by Lady Julia Chance, whose house, Orchards, had been designed by Lutyens in 1899 and whose work appears in a number of Lutyens and Jekyll gardens.

"Water takes its highest place in garden architecture when it determines the complete design of an enclosed space, such as the pool garden at Marsh Court," wrote Jekyll and Weaver in *Gardens for Small Country Houses.* "No scheme contrived within so small a compass could exceed in richness of effect this combination of steps, paving, pool, and balustrade."[11] Lutyens and Jekyll created many variations on Marsh Court's water garden in their later work, including Hestercombe, Folly Farm, and Gledstone Hall, where it makes its final appearance.

By 1905 Lutyens was the most fashionable society architect in the country, with many houses already built or underway. **Millmead,** completed that year, showed "how perfect a thing a little country house on a tiny plot of ground can be, and how a 'sordid half acre' can be transformed into an earthly paradise."[12] Gertrude Jekyll had spotted the vacant lot in Bramley, Surrey, where some old cottages had been demolished several years earlier, and saw the possibilities of building "the best small house in the whole neighborhood."[13] What struck her about the spot, despite years of rubbish accumulation and overgrown weeds, was that it was within sight of the woods of her childhood home in Bramley, where she had spent many carefree days romping. The site, a little more than a half acre, was long and narrow (75' by 400') and sloped rather awkwardly down to a marshy millmead and brook. She engaged Lutyens to design the house, while she busied herself with laying out a garden. The house that Lutyens designed was no longer in the Surrey Vernacular style of Munstead Wood and Orchards, but in a Georgian style, "rather over-windowed," according to architectural critic H. Avray Tipping.[14]

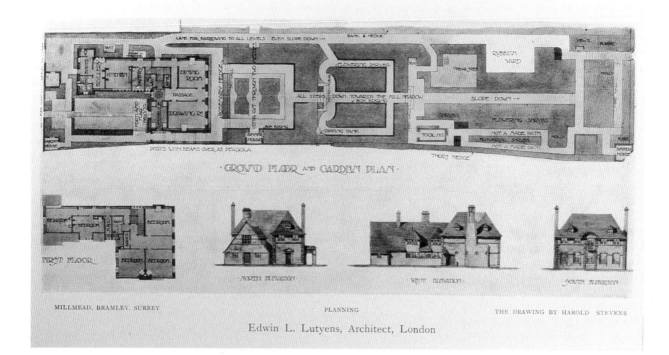

·GROUND FLOOR AND GARDEN PLAN·

·FIRST FLOOR· · NORTH ELEVATION · · WEST ELEVATION · · SOUTH ELEVATION ·

MILLMEAD, BRAMLEY, SURREY PLANNING THE DRAWING BY HAROLD STEVENS

Edwin L. Lutyens, Architect, London

The modest L-shaped house took up almost the entire width of the site and since it was located on a busy village street, like Deanery Garden, they decided to build a high enclosure wall. Like the wall at Munstead Wood, it is constructed of local bargate stone with tile coping. Where the wall ended in the back, due to the steeply sloping site, yew hedges continued the high enclosure. An opening in the wall on the street leads to a small forecourt, and a paved walk leads to the front entrance. A narrow, five-foot-wide walkway between the west side of the house and the enclosure wall provides access to the main garden on the sunny, south side of the house. "The planting in the forecourt is kept rather quiet, with plenty of green foliage," wrote Jekyll and Weaver. "The flowers are of a modest type, such as columbines and campanulas, [the intention being] green and quiet in anticipation of a riot of bright blossom in the main garden on the sunny side of the house."[15]

Jekyll divided the long, sloping garden into four terraces, starting with the relatively level area nearest to the house, where there was a rose garden with a central sundial, and ending with the thicket at the bottom near the mill stream. Jekyll admitted that the problems of the ground being a long

Edwin Lutyens, Millmead, Bramley, Surrey, drawing by Harold Stevens (from Sparrow, *Our Homes,* 1909). Author's Collection

Edwin Lutyens, Summerhouse in garden at Millmead, c. 1912. Country Life Picture Library

Edwin Lutyens, Folly Farm, Berkshire, 1985

strip required "judicious management of each succeeding level, so that each should have individuality and distinctive interest, and yet that there should be a comfortable sense of general cohesion."[16] Each compartment was delineated with low stone dry walls; profusely planted with fragrant, sun-loving plants, such as lavender; and gentle steps leading from one level to the next. The largest area, near the bottom, was given over to ebullient flower borders and ornamental fruit trees, so that from the bottom of the garden one could view the house through an impressionistic blur of flowers and foliage.

Even though the property was relatively modest in size, it included three summerhouses, the most impressive of which is located on the upper garden terrace on axis with the sundial in the rose garden. From here one could enjoy the distant views of Jekyll's childhood woodlands. She never lived in this house, as it was built as a speculative venture, but Millmead is an excellent example of Jekyll's skillful planning on a challenging site, encompassing both formal elements and informality, in the true spirit of the Arts and Crafts Movement.

In many ways Folly Farm represents the culmination of the Lutyens and Jekyll partnership, for many of the ideas that they had experimented with for years matured here. Folly Farm also represents a transition from the Arts and Crafts to the Modern movements in garden design, presaging Hidcote and Sissinghurst in its series of compartmentalized "rooms." It successfully combines vestiges of the "old" and the "new" and "newer," and like many gardens of the early twentieth century, it represents a continuum linking it to the present day. Folly Farm has had a variety of owners (but only one architect), each of whom has left an imprint, but even today it is considered the best preserved of all the Lutyens and Jekyll gardens still in private ownership.

Located in Sulhamstead, Berkshire, Folly Farm started out as a modest timber-framed farmhouse with ancillary barn buildings. In 1905, H. H. Cochrane asked Lutyens to design an addition to convert it into a country house. For this addition, which turned out to be far grander than the original cottage, Lutyens designed a storybook William and Mary style

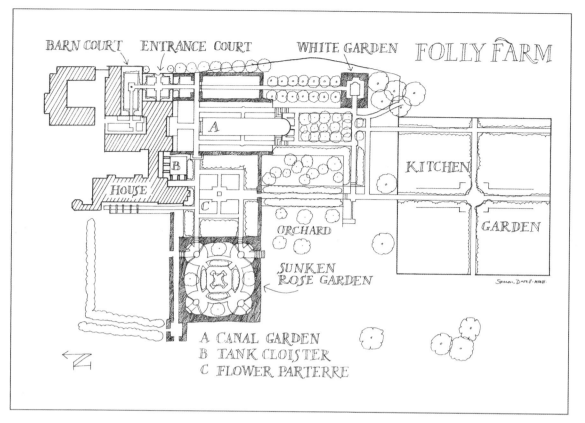

Simon Dorrell, *Garden plan for Folly Farm,* 2003

house, built in a soft gray brick with distinctive red brick trim. A symmetrical H-shaped house, it is a superb example of Lutyens's "Wrennaissance" period, inspired by late-seventeenth-century buildings by Sir Christopher Wren. As part of the commission, he designed a series of courts to tie together the old and new buildings, with flagstone paths laid in a herringbone brick pattern, similar to those at Marsh Court. For these new courts, Jekyll's borders were in a feathery cottage style, with fragrant lavender, dianthus, and roses. The new entrance court, with brick garden walls and arches, called for more formality, with an emphasis on textural green foliage. Jekyll planted a rhododendron walk to separate the village street from the house and laid out traditional grass lawns flanked by flower borders on the main façade of the new building. In all it was an attractive, but not exceptional, scheme.

The gardens at Folly Farm owe their fame to the period of the second owner, Zachary Merton, for whom Lutyens designed another addition in 1912. His fanciful barnlike structure to the west of the brick building reverts to the architect's

Edwin Lutyens, *Sunken rose parterre at Folly Farm,* 1990

earlier Vernacular style, with its exaggerated roof line swooping down to cover a buttressed cloister. With the exception of the barn court, the earlier gardens were replaced with a bolder, less conventional theme.[17] The new scheme included three different water gardens. The first, and most dramatic, a Dutch-inspired canal, modeled after seventeenth-century examples that were popular in English gardens, replaced the grass panel in front of the 1905 "Dutch" addition.[18] From the elevated water works and bridge at the far end of the canal, a feature derived from Deanery Garden, one could see the reflection of the house in the long pool.

A second water garden, a square tank tucked into the L of the cloistered loggia, also functioned as a reflecting pool. Jekyll planted the narrow borders along the edge with spikey water-loving plants, such as iris and arum. The third, and most dramatic, is a sunken water parterre planted with roses and "floating islands" of lavender, hidden behind high yew hedges. This garden served as the grand finale, with Lutyens's halfmoon steps, curving stone paths, and herringbone brick detail. It was an architectural garden in its most ingenious configuration.

In his review of Folly Farm for *Country Life*, Hussey mused, "Probably, every man, and certainly every woman, at intervals in his life lays out gardens if only in the fertile soil of imagination."[19] Folly Farm owes its great significance to the way it was laid out, as a series of interlinking "rooms," each with a special vista to the house. It is also a garden of axial viewpoints in the manner of the great formal gardens of the seventeenth century. The water parterre and the canal garden are linked by a square formal garden in the middle that is surrounded by borders filled with blue and purple flowers. The main cross-axial path centered on the 1912 addition leads from this formal garden to a large walled kitchen garden. Part of the magic of Folly Farm's gardens is the network of linear yew hedges that define each "room" and cut off the view from one area to the next. The idea of compartmentalized "garden rooms"—progressing from one experience to the next—would become the hallmark of gardens of the modern era.

In the 1920s and 1930s it took six gardeners to maintain Folly Farm, and in later years the plantings were simplified or removed.[20] The fact that plants could be changed and new areas be planned owes much to Lutyens's and Jekyll's brilliant scheme that reflected years of expertise. No other architects of the Arts and Crafts Movement had the benefit of such sympathetic and skillful collaboration.

Edwin Lutyens's *Halfmoon steps at Folly Farm,* 1990

Chapter 9 | Beyond the Borders.

In an article about a Scottish house for *Country Life*, Lawrence Weaver remarked that "the English architectural critic, on crossing the Tweed, travels into what is almost a foreign land."[1] Nevertheless, Scotland was home to one of the most distinguished of all the Arts and Crafts architects, Robert Stodart Lorimer (1864–1929), whose houses and gardens were founded on a centuries-old tradition of Scots tower houses and their walled gardens. Like Lutyens, Lorimer's architecture was championed in the pages of *Country Life* and both architects shared a passion for materials and a romantic vision of a garden.[2] With the exception of four of Lorimer's houses in England, for which Gertrude Jekyll designed the gardens, the architect laid out the gardens for his commissions.[3]

Scotland's attitudes to domestic architecture were significantly different from those in England. Whereas the English house centered on the horizontality of the hall, in Scotland it was the verticality of the tower. Most of the significant castles in Scotland owe their origins to the late seventeenth century, from which Lorimer derived his own style. Garden traditions were also different from those in England, mainly due to the absence of the eighteenth-century landscape movement that obliterated many older English gardens. Because Scotland's climate is varied—milder on the West Coast, which benefits from the Gulf Stream, and windy and damp on the East Coast, which faces the North Sea—Scottish gardens relied on enclosure walls and hedges for windbreaks. Kitchen gardens (with stoves inside the walls to help ripen fruit in a short growing season), topiary, and splendid examples of garden architecture were hallmarks of these gardens.

Gardening arts blossomed in Scotland in the seventeenth century, but little survives prior to that period that is the equal of England's Hampton Court. Edzell Castle, perhaps the most romantic ruin in Scotland today, has one of the earliest extant gardens. Located near Forfar, on the East Coast, it was once a wealthy Scots laird's house built in the early sixteenth century. The garden, dating from 1604, consists of a walled courtyard of approximately a half-acre, with a two-story summerhouse in one corner. Unusual rectangular recesses hollowed out in the walls are thought to resemble a heraldic *fess chequé* relating to the Lindsay family's coat-of-arms. These recesses provide pockets for plants, and circular openings in the walls provide nesting areas for birds.

Jekyll and Weaver commented that it was a device "worthy of adoption in modern walled gardens."[4] The magnificent enclosure walls also have bas-relief sculptural panels representing the planetary deities, the liberal arts, and cardinal virtues. In all, this paradise garden played a significant role in how Lorimer configured his gardens.

Robert Lorimer, who was born in Edinburgh and educated at Edinburgh University (where his father was a professor), came from an artists' family. After training with an architect in Edinburgh, Lorimer worked in G. F. Bodley's London office for several years before returning home to establish his own practice. While in London, Lorimer discovered the Morris circle and was soon swept up in the Arts and Crafts Movement. Like Gimson and other craftsman-architects, Lorimer experimented with the allied arts, such as plasterwork and embroidery, and designed baronial-style furniture that was made by local craftsmen.

As his biographer Christopher Hussey noted, Lorimer had an extraordinary grasp of detail, a craftsman's approach to architecture, and a deep understanding of Scottish traditional architecture. "He had a rare faculty of renewing the original character of an old building and yet changing it with his own personality," he observed.[5] Until the 1920s, Lorimer designed a large number of Scottish country houses with outstanding decorative interiors executed by local craftsmen.

Lorimer applied Blomfield's call for formalism to the heritage of Scottish gardens, its traditional layout, furnishings, and garden architecture freely modeled after the layout at Edzell Castle. Lorimer thought that a garden should be "in tune with the house . . . a sort of sanctuary . . . to wander in, to cherish, to dream through undisturbed . . . a little pleasaunce of the soul, by whose wicket the world can be shut."[6] His ideal garden was a walled enclosure, with "little gardens within the garden, the 'month's garden,' the herb garden, the yew alley . . . the kitchen garden [with] great intersecting walks of shaven grass, . . . borders of brightest flowers backed by low espaliers hanging with shining apples."[7] Lorimer's romantic vision is strikingly similar to Morris's at Red House.

Lorimer's first foray into garden design came during his adolescent years at Kellie Castle, near Fife, where the family

Opposite:
Edzell Castle, Angus, 1987

Below:
Simon Dorrell, *Garden plan for Kellie Castle,* 2003

Overleaf:
Robert Lorimer, *Kellie Castle, Fife,* 1987

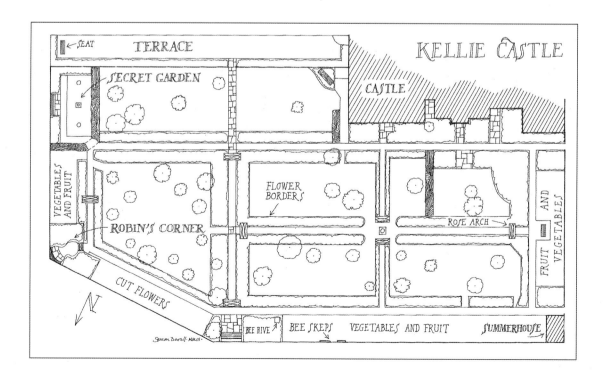

spent their summers. In 1878, Lorimer's father rescued the desolate seventeenth-century tower house, then a roofless ruin in the middle of a turnip field. To celebrate the successful remodeling of the house, a Latin inscription was added over the entrance door that translates, "This mansion snatched from rooks and owls is dedicated to honest repose from labour." When the Lorimer family arrived, only the bare outlines of the one-acre garden still existed, as it was seriously overgrown and the walls were crumbling. "The garden [was] still encircled by a tumbledown wall," wrote Robert's youngest sister, Louise, "a wilderness of neglected gooseberry bushes, gnarled apple trees, and old world roses, which struggled through the weeds, summer after summer, with a sweet persistence."[8] The Lorimers set out to refurbish the garden, rebuilding walls and dividing the one-acre space into compartments, with a long grass walk and a circular center for an astrolabe with a ship on top. "It converted that part, overloaded with gooseberry bushes, into an orderly and stately place."[9] Robert designed two new enclosures, including a small garden enclosed by yew hedges with topiaries, and a small garden house in the northeast corner of the garth that quickly took on the age and appearance of the castle because of the use of old slates from a farm building.

It was Louise Lorimer who was the most actively involved with the garden, planting and maintaining it for many years. Gertrude Jekyll's account of Kellie in *Some English Gardens* leaves no doubt that it was an exemplary garden of roses and their companion plantings. "How the flowers grow in these northern gardens," she exclaimed. "Here they must needs grow tall to be in scale with the high box edging [and] this is just the garden for the larger plants, [especially] single Hollyhocks in big free groups, and double Hollyhocks too."[10] Since the early 1990s the garden, now a property of the National Trust for Scotland, has been cultivated organically, with dozens of varieties of vegetables in addition to the garden flowers.[11]

One of the reasons that Lorimer returned to Scotland in 1892 was that he had received his first commission, to restore a ruinous late-sixteenth-century castle near Leuchars, in Fife, on the East Coast.[12] Earlshall had been purchased the previous year by Robert Mackenzie, a family friend whose interest in the Arts and Crafts Movement led him to the young architect. Lorimer completely rehabilitated the dilapidated castle, adding ornate interiors with paneling carved with Morris-inspired floral patterns. He also added a two-storey tool house adorned with carved stone monkeys on the roof in one corner of the garden enclosure as well as a new gate lodge.

Robert Lorimer, Topiary garden at Earlshall, Fife, 1987

Part of Lorimer's charge was to create a garden that echoed the antiquity of the tower house. Little remained in the original enclosure, which was used for grazing livestock and surrounded by fourteen acres of parkland—a Robinsonian wild garden—that provided the ideal prelude to the garden he envisioned within the walls. "The natural park comes up to the walls of the house on the one side," **Lorimer** wrote, "on the other you stroll out into the garden enclosed. . . . an intentional and deliberate piece of careful design, a place that is garnished and nurtured with the tenderest care [and that] marries with the demesne that lies beyond."[13] The new gateway in the wall includes the inscription: "Here shall ye see no enemy but winter and rough weather."

L. Rome Guthrie,
Earlshall, Fifeshire, drawing (from Triggs, *Formal Gardens in England and Scotland,* 1902, Plate 87). Author's Collection

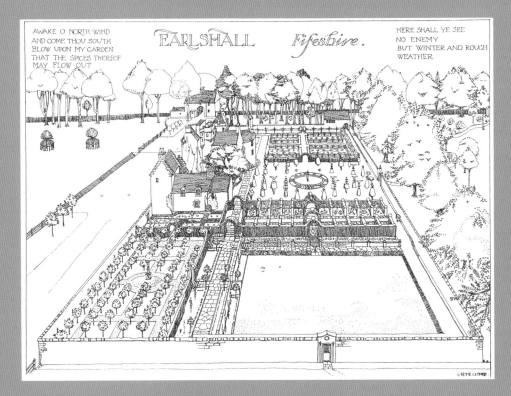

AWAKE O NORTH WIND AND COME THOU SOUTH BLOW UPON MY GARDEN THAT THE SPICES THEREOF MAY FLOW OUT

EARLSHALL Fifeshire.

HERE SHALL YE SEE NO ENEMY BUT WINTER AND ROUGH WEATHER

A bird's-eye view of the garden shows the garden enclosed. Along the entry drive and the long grass ride that runs parallel to the west boundary wall of the enclosure, Lorimer planted a double allée of pleached lime trees. For the enclosure itself, he divided the space into five compartments, each defined by clipped holly or yew hedges. The northern section was allocated to a four-square fruit and vegetable garden, with espaliered fruit trees on the walls, wide grass walks in the center, and a line of lime trees on the eastern boundary. The southern section was divided into an orchard and bowling green or croquet lawn. A cross-axial grass walk leading to a semicircular stone arbor in the eastern wall was enclosed by high arched hedges, with ten battlemented yew alcoves filled with roses, azaleas, and fuchsia.

The main feature of the garden is the extraordinary topiary pleasance, positioned between the vegetable garden and the yew walk. Planted in four diagonal crosses, it was designed to be viewed from the house. To give the topiary garden a well-established appearance, Lorimer specified yews from an abandoned Edinburgh garden that were then clipped into cake-stands, birds, and other traditional topiary forms.[14] The fanciful garden exuded the old-world appearance of a seventeenth-century Scottish garden, providing a worthy complement to the old house. Thus, in his first commission, Lorimer brought the tradition of old Scottish gardens back to life, and in so doing had invented a style that made his name. Earlshall represents the most magical, and successful, of his gardens, encapsulating all that he valued in the concept of house and garden enclosed.

* * *

Wales, separated from England by the Severn and a boundary line meandering from Chepstow to Chester, abounds in historic parks and gardens, although most are well-kept secrets. Bodnant, Powis Castle, Erddig, and Plas Newydd are some of the better-known gardens of the eighteeenth and nineteenth centuries, but hidden among the hills and vales are some remarkable examples from the Arts and Crafts era.[15] In addition to Mallows's Craig-y-Parc and Mawson's Dyffryn near Cardiff, there are several by the architectural writer H. Avray Tipping in Monmouthshire, and the visionary architect Clough Williams-Ellis in North Wales.

Henry Avray Tipping (1855–1933) adopted Wales for his country homes. A man of independent means with a first in modern history from Oxford, Tipping was a connoisseur of architecture and antiques. He was also a passionate and knowledgeable gardener, having been given his first garden when he was seven years old. Most unusually for a historian, he was the author of a book about practical gardening, based on his newspaper columns. Tipping's reputation rests primarily on hundreds of definitive articles he wrote on houses for *Country Life,* beginning around 1907. Christopher Hussey observed that "Tipping brought to the writing of the articles an historical knowledge and an insistence on accuracy that gave them a new authoritativeness."[16] In addition to setting a standard for *Country Life,* Tipping compiled numerous books, including the multivolume *In English Homes, English Homes, Gardens Old and New,* and one of his most popular publications, *English Gardens.*

Tipping's obsession with architecture and gardens played out in a succession of country homes, each one of which reflected his unerring eye for design and ability to capture a mood. When queried about the excessive costs incurred for one of them, he retorted, "You see I do not care to keep racehorses or dancing ladies. I prefer to spend my money on walls."[17] Although he maintained a London residence, like *Country Life* editor Edward Hudson, who also had a succession of homes, Tipping yearned for the country where he could immerse himself in architectural minutiae and gardens.

Tipping's first major home in Wales was Mathern Palace, a medieval residence in ruinous condition that had once belonged to the Bishops of Llandaff. He bought Mathern in 1894, and after carefully restoring it commented that despite the grandeur of its name, his only aim had been to create "a quiet home where the simple life may be led."[18] Unlike an architect, he used a light hand in the restoration, repairing what could be saved without interfering with "the patina of age."[19] The flat site and the old farmyard enclosures provided an ideal setting for a new garden to complement the picturesque old house. Within the ancient walls he laid out a series of enclosures, with a bowling green, yew hedges, grass walks, and topiaries clipped into forms of foxes, cocks, and pheasants. "Topiary work is rather like a drink," he wrote. "Against it there are ardent prohibitionists such as William Robinson [and] outbursts of intoxicated license." He recommended the middle course of "moderate indulgence."[20] On the more sloping portion of the site, Tipping created informal rock and water gardens. In all, it was an enchanting garden, reflecting a distillation of the theories of Robinson and Jekyll.

Tipping soon became restless for another challenge, which he found nearby at Mounton House, where he began developing a naturalistic woodland garden in the steep valley and limestone gorge around 1900. A young Chepstow architect,

H. Avray Tipping, Pool and pergola at Mounton House, Chepstow, *1915. Country Life Picture Library*

Overleaf: *H. Avray Tipping and E. C. Francis,* Wyndcliffe Court, Monmouthshire, *1993*

Clough Williams-Ellis, Garden house and water garden at Cornwell Manor, Oxfordshire, 1993

Eric Carwardine Francis (1887–1976), a pupil of Guy Dawber and assistant to Detmar Blow, designed the house perched high on the cliff, with views of the Bristol Channel and the Mendip Hills. Together they created formal terraces around the house rivaling those at Deanery Garden in ingenuity and visual appeal. Near the house he made a long bowling green and in another area, a reflecting pool and pergola with massive piers smothered with climbing roses and wisteria. There were more elaborate plantings in the surrounding paved gardens. To the west of the house lay the precipitous descent into the stream garden below.[21]

In 1922 Francis designed High Glanau, on a site chosen for its spectacular views over Gwent. "The lie of the land," Tipping wrote, "happily suggested a dovetailing instead of a rigid boundary between the wild and the formal."[22] His design allowed one to look down from the house and its formal terraces to a lily pool at the bottom of the steps or out at the view. "There is nothing really wild at Glanau," Tipping wrote. "There are woodlands . . . more or less left to native vegetation, more or less swept and garnished. It is gardening, but with nature kept in the forefront of set purpose."[23]

Wyndcliffe Court, Monmouthshire, built by Francis in 1922 for Charles Clay, is one of only a handful of Tipping's gardens that remains largely unchanged today. The modest house, sited on a bluff commanding views of the Severn estuary, is complemented by gardens that represent the impeccable planning principles of the Arts and Crafts tradition.[24] The terraces, bowling green, topiary, and sunken water garden dip deeply into Tipping's favorite vocabulary. In the topiary terrace just below the house, a semi-circular pool tucked beneath the wall is reminiscent of those designed by Lutyens for Hestercombe and Deanery Garden. The bowling green on the next level down sports spirals of hand-clipped yew topiaries, and a few steps below is Tipping's sunken garden, with a central pool and surrounding borders that takes its cue from the one at Hampton Court. A nicely detailed two-storey summerhouse in the far corner of the sunken garden draws the eye to the distant landscape. Wyndcliffe Court is remarkable for its cozy, domestic scale, encapsulating Tipping's vision of house and garden totally dovetailed.

* * *

Clough Williams-Ellis (1883–1978) was one of the last great architects to take up the cause of the Arts and Crafts Movement. An artist by nature, he had a lifelong curiosity about architecture and boundless energy. After Trinity College, Cambridge, he trained briefly at the Architectural Association in London in 1902, but his family was skeptical of his choice of career, for architecture was thought of "as a gentlemanly hobby for the well-to-do [and] little better than plumbing as a career."[25] In particular, he was fascinated by rural cottages and old-time building methods. Like many Arts and Crafts architects, he had a fondness for regional materials, in particular the rough stone of his homeland in Wales.[26] In the Arts and Crafts tradition, he produced many beautiful watercolor perspectives and renderings for his projects, although many were lost in a fire in 1951.[27]

In 1906 he set up an office in London, designing model cottages and small residences in various architectural styles, and remodeling old houses; after World War I he branched out into other areas, including village design. In addition to architecture, Williams-Ellis had a lifelong passion for land conservation and preservation of the rural environment in Wales, where his family had their roots. In a curious book entitled England and the Octopus (1928), he wrote about urban sprawl (the octopus) encroaching on the rural countryside.[28] During his long lifetime, he developed many important friendships among architects, including Frank Lloyd Wright, who visited Williams-Ellis in 1956 on his only visit to his ancestral country.

Some of his better-known residential projects include a remodeling of Llangoed Hall in Powys (now a country house hotel) and Oare House in Wiltshire, for which he designed some delightful garden benches that are illustrated in Jekyll and Hussey's Garden Ornament, with the comment, "they are strong and simple, yet full of amusing life," that sums up Williams-Ellis's approach to architecture.[29] In 1937 he restored Cornwell village in Oxfordshire for an American client, Mrs. Anthony Gillson, who gave him carte blanche in the nine-acre garden at Cornwell Manor as well. With the exception of his own home in Wales, this is probably one of his most complete surviving gardens. He linked the village and the old manor house with a watercourse that meanders through the village and becomes more formalized in the house grounds, widening into several pools and a long canal. He also extended the view of the house from the public road through a line of trees in the park opposite. On the terrace near the house, a small garden with clipped Portuguese laurels and a fiddler statue in the center add a note of formality in contrast to the rock and bog gardens surrounding the lower watercourse.

Williams-Ellis's most lasting contribution, where all of his diverse ideas coalesced, was the creation of Portmeirion, a model village built on the coast of Snowdonia between 1926 and 1976. Plas Brondanw, Williams-Ellis's home nearby, has one of the best-preserved Arts and Crafts gardens in Britain, one that reinforces the critical relationship of house, garden, and surrounding landscape. As Hussey noted, "[I]t is at Brondanw, much better than at Portmeirion, its fantastic offshoot, that we can see the original fundamental Clough."[30] When he was twenty-five years old, and in his "antiquarian phase," he received Plas Brondanw as a gift from his family. The gray stone house, dating from the seventeenth century, had long been abandoned. Over the next decades, Williams-Ellis poured his energy and income into rehabilitating the old house and creating a garden on the steeply falling ground. Beginning in 1908, he used the local bluish-purple stone to build walls and terraces around the house, and added a gate lodge and orangery around 1914. Plas Brondanw was substantially rebuilt in 1951 after a fire destroyed the home and most of Williams-Ellis's records.

Above:
Simon Dorrell, *Main axis at Plas Brondanw, with a view to Cnicht,* ink drawing (*Hortus,* Summer 2001)

Right:
Clough Williams-Ellis, *East terrace at Cornwell Manor,* 1993

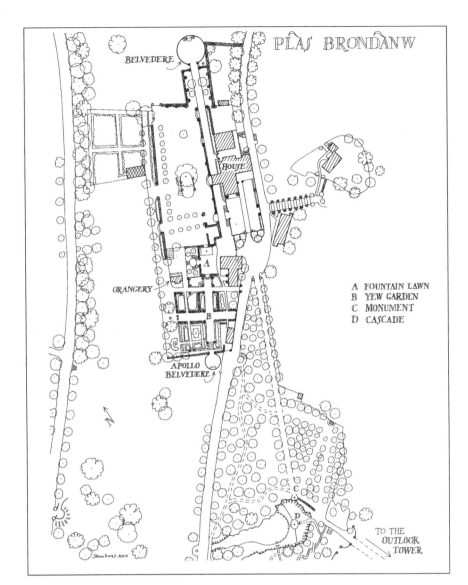

A FOUNTAIN LAWN
B YEW GARDEN
C MONUMENT
D CASCADE

Left:
Simon Dorrell, Garden plan for Plas Brondanw, 2003

Opposite:
Clough Williams-Ellis, Flower gardens and orangery at Plas Brondanw, Gwynedd, 2002

The garden is ingenious for its control in providing vistas to the Snowdonia mountain range, notably the Cnicht peak. Two main axes, a walkway to the northeast that terminates in the belvedere roundel overlooking Cnicht, and the other to the Apollo belvedere overlooking the quarry pool, are lined with green hedges or topiary, with little emphasis on flowers that would detract from the panoramic views. The flower garden, filled primarily with blue hydrangeas and blue-green hostas, is hidden behind the hedged compartments. A cross-axis in the yew garden looks to a carefully framed view of Moel Hebog in the distance. Delicate iron gates are painted a special blue-green that sizzles against the green lawn. An oblong fountain pool, with a statue of a fireboy by sculptor Gertrude Knoblock, benches, clipped topiaries, arched hedges, Italian cypresses, and statuary accentuate the strongly architectural layout.[31] Like the homes of other proponents of the Arts and Crafts Movement, Clough Williams-Ellis's Plas Brondanw provides the best expression of his individuality.

Chapter 10 | Color in the Flower Garden.

A heightened sensitivity to planting composition and use of color was a key component of Arts and Crafts gardens. In theory, the floral furnishings for outdoor rooms needed to be as carefully considered as the architectural elements. In place of carpets of annuals, designers sought soothing, more informal solutions by selecting plants for their compatibility with one another. This artistic approach to planting was taken by artist-gardeners who were thoroughly versed in design and color theory, rather than by architects who delegated planting to nurserymen or horticultural advisers. Taking their cue from William Morris and William Robinson, who sang the praises of perennials, artist-gardeners looked to a more sensitive palette of plants and colors than Victorian gardeners.

Gertrude Jekyll's agility in combining form, texture, and color in her borders is legendary, but other artist-gardeners advocated this approach also. Like Jekyll, Alfred Parsons (1847–1920) was an artist and an accomplished garden designer. A regular exhibitor at the Royal Academy and the New English Art Club, he was also president of the Royal Society of Painters in Water Colours, an indication of the high regard in which he was held. His illustrations enhance many of Robinson's books and journals, including *The Wild Garden*, for which he illustrated a special edition. Parsons lived in Broadway, a picture-book village in Worcestershire, where he was part of the Broadway Group of American illustrators for *Harper's Magazine* that centered on artists Edwin Austin Abbey (with whom he shared a home) and Frank Millet. Parsons once shared a studio with John Singer Sargent, who painted *Carnation, Lily, Lily, Rose* while based in Broadway in 1885.[1] Henry James, another Broadway habitué, commented that Parsons's work "forms the richest illustration of the English landscape that is offered us to-day. . . . One would like to retire to another planet with a box of Mr. Parsons's drawings, and be homesick there for the pleasant places they commemorate."[2]

Parsons's own garden at Luggers Hill, near Broadway, was quintessential Arts and Crafts in both its planning and furnishings, with high green hedges shaped as battlements, topiary, beautifully composed flower borders, a picturesque summerhouse, and a rose garden.[3] Parsons's paintings of Broadway gardens attest to his fine-tuned color sensitivity as well as a botanical accuracy that outdistances most garden painters of the era who were less horticulturally

inclined. While based in Broadway, Parsons designed numerous gardens, such as stage actress Mary Anderson de
Navarro's Court Farm that was as famous for its topiary peacocks and flower borders as it was for its visitors.[4] The timber-framed house, with thatched roof and dovecote, was covered in a "whirlwind of climbing roses," one of Parsons's
signature effects.[5]

One of Parsons's most visible gardens is Wightwick Manor,
Wolverhampton, West Midlands. Designed by architect
Edward Ould (1852–1909) in a picturesque half-timbered old
English style derivative of Shaw, Wightwick is famous for its
collections of the work of the Morris firm and Pre-Raphaelite
artists assembled by the Mander family. In 1899 Parsons and
his partner, Walter Partridge, laid out the upper gardens near
the house, a formal rose garden surrounded by hedges and
topiaried yews, and a long walk bordered with flowers.
Clipped yew hedges, topiary peacocks, picture-perfect bor-

ders, and cascades of roses typify Parsons's style. His most
famous illustrations are those for Ellen Willmott's book, *The
Genus Rosa* (1910–14), containing 132 illustrations of rose
species described by the author. Although the book was a
financial and artistic disaster, because Willmott ignored
Parsons's recommendations regarding papers and printers,
the resulting paintings are a legacy to both client and artist.[6]

Ellen Ann Willmott (1858–1934) was beautiful, intelligent,
and wealthy, but not financially savvy. Independently wealthy
from the age of eighteen, she overextended her resources
managing three gardens: Warley Place, Essex, where she kept
over 100 gardeners busy for years; Tresserve, in Aix-les-Bains,
France; and Boccanegra, in Ventimiglia, Italy.[7] Along with
Robinson and Jekyll, Willmott was one of the three most
important gardeners of the era. All three received the coveted
Victoria Medal of Honour from the Royal Horticultural
Society. Jekyll thought Willmott was the greatest of living gar-

deners, and Robinson had boundless respect for her accomplishments as a hybridizer. There are few gardens in Britain without *Eryngium giganteum*, or "Miss Willmott's Ghost," known for its startling blue color.

In its heyday, Warley Place was fifty-five acres in extent, filled with rockeries, roses, perennials, and naturalized sweeps of snowdrops, crocus, tulips, daffodils, and other bulbs that Willmott hybridized. While still a young woman, she commissioned an extensive alpine garden from the Backhouse firm in York, and from there her passion for plants and gardens grew unabated until her death as a near-destitute woman. Little remains of any of her gardens, but her book, *Warley Garden in Spring and Summer*, records that garden in its most splendid state.

The Manor House, Sutton Courtenay, in Berkshire, is another once-splendid garden associated with a keen horticulturist and brilliant designer. The home of Norah Lindsay

(1876–1948), it exuded an air of spontaneity in its plantings, "as if the flowers and trees had chosen their own positions," to quote Mrs. Lindsay.[8] She laid out the gardens as a series of rooms to complement the low, half-timbered house. The Long Garden, punctuated with fastigate yews and soft mounds of boxwood, was filled with bold groups of lupines, anchusas, mulleins, followed by thalictrums, hollyhocks, campanulas, and other English flowers planted in big informal drifts. The color scheme, while appearing deceptively carefree, was carefully considered. The rich blues, deep purples, pinks, and yellows were kept separate from the "hot scarlet of the sizzling great poppies, the burning alstroemerias and all the metallic golds of the rudbeckias and sunflowers," noted Lindsay. An American visitor commented that Lindsay's colors were soft greens, gray, buff-violet, and softest salmon.[9] Lindsay, a colorful, if not eccentric woman, designed gardens for the cream of the aristocracy, including the Duke of Windsor at Fort Belvedere,

Windsor, but her most famous association is that with Lawrence Johnston's Hidcote Manor.

Gertrude Jekyll's Munstead Wood, which has happily survived, was a proving ground for nearly 400 garden commissions, the most famous of which were those done in collaboration with Lutyens. Undoubtedly Jekyll began designing gardens in response to many requests to supply the special plants she grew at Munstead Wood. Her notebooks detail shipments of plants to dozen of clients' gardens, ranging from small ones owned by friends to large, complex ones designed with Lutyens. Jekyll was omnivorous in her appreciation of plants, commenting that there were no "bad" plants, only plants badly used. In the 1920s, when she was in her eighties and nearly blind, she designed borders from her memory of hundreds of plants, their colors, textures, fragrances, and habits.

Sometimes she adjusted her planting style to suit the needs of the architect or the client, as was the case at Hestercombe, the landmark garden she and Lutyens designed in Somerset. Even though Hestercombe has many familiar Jekyll plants, the dramatic arrangements are not the informal cottage-garden style on which she had built her reputation. Tipping commented in 1908, four years after the garden was designed, that "Hestercombe is rather too much an architect's and rather too little a gardener's garden." There was too much of "that rather dull plant, the grey-leaved stachys."[10] Lutyens's great classical garden with rustic detailing is somewhat of an anomaly, because it lacks the appropriate house—Hestercombe was a homely Victorian of the most banal sort—and his architectural components are classical, not Arts and Crafts, in spirit. Lutyens's blending of local stone, orange ashlar and rose-pink shale, in the buildings, paths, water rills, and pools, however, reflects his vernacular sensibilities.

Jekyll's plantings at Hestercombe take their theme from her gray, pink, and white borders at Munstead Wood that were equally suited to the warm tones of the Somerset stone. In the Dutch Garden, she has composed a symphony of grays with santolina, dwarf lavender, rosemary, and *Yucca filamentosa*, edged with miles of *Stachys* (lambs' ears). Beds in the central part of the garden are filled with peonies, lilies, and delphiniums, and edged with her signature *Bergenia cordifolia* foliage. A gray walk is devoted exclusively to gray foliage and cool-toned pink and lavender plants with white accents. Unquestionably, Hestercombe was conceived as a showpiece in its day, but it represents only one side of Jekyll's planting genius.

Left: *Alfred Parsons* (1847–1920), *Warley Place, Essex,* watercolor. Christopher Wood Gallery, London

Opposite: *Norah Lindsay's Long Garden at the Manor House at Sutton Courtenay, Berkshire,* 1930. Country Life Picture Library

Overleaf: *Gertrude Jekyll, Gray foliage in the Dutch Garden at Hestercombe, Somerset,* 1990

The Manor House at Upton Grey, in Hampshire, is one of the best examples of Jekyll's skills as a planting artist and a garden designer, displaying her versatility in planning both formal and wild gardens for a small property. It takes many quotations from Munstead Wood, Hestercombe, and Millmead. The Manor House was the former home of Charles Holme, founder of *The Studio*, who lived there for twenty years after moving from Morris's Red House in 1902. Ernest Newton designed a comfortable Edwardian family home around the core of an old Tudor farmhouse, and the design of the four and one-half acres of ground fell to Gertrude Jekyll.

On the east side of the house, she designed a formal garden within the framework of yew hedges, converting the grass slopes into four descending terraces, each defined with low, dry-stone walls filled with rock plants in soft pinks and grays. A small pergola that links the house to the steps leading to the gardens below, is covered with roses, clematis, and other vines. The rose garden, divided into geometric beds with square stone pads, is simply planted with roses and peonies and softly edged with *Stachys*. On the lower levels are a wide bowling green and a tennis lawn enclosed with ornamental trees and shrubs. Surrounding borders are planted with *Yucca filamentosa*, *Yucca gloriosa*, *Bergenia cordifolia*, and other familiar Jekyll plants. In contrast with the soft coloring of the rose garden, the main borders are more dramatically colored, following the same ideas of color gradation as in the main border at Munstead Wood. A large wild garden at the west front of the house follows Robinsonian principles with its informal design and naturalistic plantings. Mown grass paths wind through taller grass, with rambling roses, walnut trees, and clumps of bamboo. The pond at the far end of the garden nourishes water-loving plants, and in spring, the meadows are carpeted with daffodils, snowdrops, scilla, muscari, fritillaria, anemones, hellebores, and primrose.[11]

Ernest Newton, Manor House at Upton Grey, Hampshire, 1993

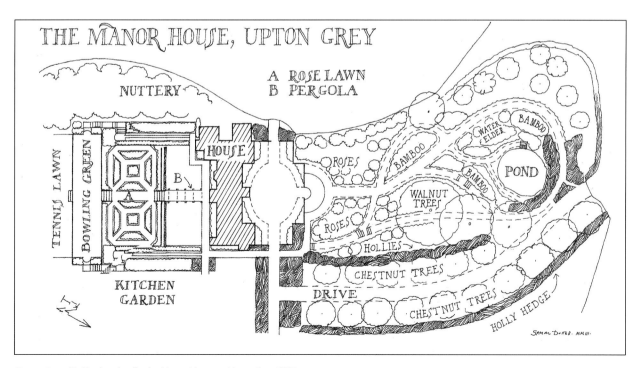

THE MANOR HOUSE, UPTON GREY

A ROSE LAWN
B PERGOLA

NUTTERY

HOUSE

TENNIS LAWN

BOWLING GREEN

KITCHEN GARDEN

ROSES

ROSES

HOLLIES

CHESTNUT TREES

DRIVE

CHESTNUT TREES

BAMBOO

BAMBOO

WATER ELDER

BAMBOO

BAMBOO

POND

WALNUT TREES

HOLLY HEDGE

SIMON DORRELL. MMIII.

Simon Dorrell, Garden plan for the Manor House at Upton Grey, 2003

Almost everyone who was interested in the finer points of garden design and horticulture read her books. *Colour in the Flower Garden* had a profound influence on writers and gardeners on both sides of the Atlantic because it is eminently readable, reflecting nearly thirty years' worth of experience in the subject, and Munstead Wood, which was used as illustrations for her ideas, was by then world famous. The book also includes planting plans for every conceivable type of border that could be used as a practical resource. There are few gardens in Britain that do not owe something to Jekyll's ideas. At Crathes Castle, a picture-book Scottish tower house in Banchory, near Aberdeen, the Burnett family married the ancient gardens with a series of color gardens directly influenced by *Colour in the Flower Garden*, including blue, white, red borders as well as a gold foliage garden, the last added by Lady Burnett in 1973. While not replicating Jekyll's borders,

those at Crathes drink of their spirit. Long before the color borders were added, Jekyll had admired the Edwardian gardens at Crathes in *Some English Gardens*, noting the excellence of their color and diversity of texture.

The eminent plantsman and botanical artist Graham Stuart Thomas (1909–2003) remarked that *Colour in the Flower Garden* had piqued his interest enough to seek a visit to Munstead Wood a year before Jekyll died. "I was spellbound," he wrote. "The gradation of tints [in the main flower border] testified to the skill of her garden staff, and to her ideas, developed from the deep study of various arts. . . . any plant which would grow well in her sandy soil was a colour in a paint-box."[12] In his long career as gardens adviser to the National Trust, he had the opportunity to put some of Jekyll's lessons to work. At Cliveden, the elegant Victorian estate of the Astor family, Thomas designed two herbaceous borders

Above:
Gertrude Jekyll, Main flower borders at the Manor House at Upton Grey, 1989

Opposite above:
Gertrude Jekyll, Rose garden at the Manor House at Upton Grey, 1993
Overleaf:
June borders at Crathes Castle, Aberdeenshire, 1990

facing each other on a wide lawn to the north of the house. One in cool colors, the other in hot, the borders successfully weave a complex tapestry of color and texture. Thomas described these borders as giving maximum color in July and August, augmented with purple clematises and yellow roses on the "hot" wall, and lavender and pink clematises and pink roses on the east-facing "cool" wall. Penelope Hobhouse, herself a noted garden designer clearly influenced by Jekyll, praised Thomas for his understanding and execution of the subtleties of her art. Jekyll's genius, wrote Hobhouse, lies in "the gradual build up of related shades and tones of colour [and] in a sure sense of what ancillary plants should be used as links to unite the whole scheme."[13]

In the 1940s, plantsman Peter Healing created a series of perennial borders in his small garden in Kemerton, near Tewkesbury. While not replicating Jekyll's Munstead Wood border, which was filled with annuals and perennials, they are equally innovative in their discerning use of color. Subtle color combinations are interwoven imaginatively with the various textures of shrubs, annuals, and hardy perennials. One border is given over to gray, silver, and white, with warm yellows and reds. A red border cleverly combines bronze, purple, and red foliage and flowers. Like the more famous color borders at Hidcote, Sissinghurst, and Tintinhull House, ingenuity in planting often takes its inspiration from books, but the results are always individual. Taken together with the local architecture and garden traditions, each in some ways is a reflection of the Arts and Crafts sensibilities to color, form, and texture.

Of the many outstanding designers today, one stands out for her romantic sense of a garden and unusual combinations of plants. Helen Dillon has created a world-famous garden in Dublin that never ceases to inspire because of its small size and suburban location. She is passionate about plants, traveling far from home to acquire unusual specimens, but the result is not a collector's garden. In creating her garden, she wrestled with how "to reconcile the collector's instinct with the desire to make a garden that is pleasant to be in. This is a challenging task because a collector's garden is all too frequently a cabinet of curiosities, a glorious confection of

plants," she wrote.[14] Jekyll opined that "the possession of a quantity of plants, however good the plants may be themselves and however ample their number, does not make a garden: it only makes a *collection*."[15] Dillon has observed that "visitors assume that one night, in a flash of creativity, I designed this garden. Not so. My method is to wait until some part of it annoys me and then take action. . . . Endless adjustments have taken place—in the paths, the shapes of the beds, and, above all, in the planting."[16]

Dillon's garden is one filled with surprises and many special effects, but her twin borders, best viewed from the window in her Georgian townhouse, literally take one's breath away. The blue border, she writes, is a "glorious muddle of different blues. . . . turquoise, sapphire, lapis lazuli." She is willing to break a few rules, even Jekyll's stern dictum that a garden with only blue flowers is senseless. "Surely the business of the blue garden is to be beautiful as well as to be blue. . . . the blues will be more telling—more purely blue—by the juxtaposition of rightly placed complementary colour."[17] With the subtle shading from blue to mauve to violet, illuminated with mounds of artemisias, Dillon has proved otherwise. Delphiniums, larkspur, monkshood, goat's rue (*Galega officinalis*), *Clematis x durandii*, *Salvia patens*, *Aster x frikartii*, and other plants swirl together as colors in a paintbox. The red border is formed mainly with foliage, such as *Heuchera* 'Pewter Moon' and *H. micrantha* 'Purple Palace'; *Berberis thunbergii* 'Atropurpurea Nana', *Rodgersia pinnata* 'Superba', and *Euphorbia dulcis* 'Chameleon' form the backbone of the border, with brilliant reds, such as *Dahlia* 'Bishop of Llandaff', making a stunning display.

The challenge of arranging these borders is endlessly fascinating, "perhaps because there's no chance whatsoever of getting it right—the more I think about it the more complicated it becomes."[18] Only those who are truly knowledgeable about plants, whether Gertrude Jekyll, Norah Lindsay, or Helen Dillon, can even begin to compose artistic borders. The architects who provided such a firm foundation for Arts and Crafts gardens would have been nowhere if there had not been dedicated horticulturists to create the plantings.

Helen Dillon, Red and blue borders, Dillon Garden, Dublin, 2000

The British Arts and Crafts Movement had a dramatic impact on European design, thanks to its widespread exposure in magazines and books as well as the strong presence of its founding leaders. In America, architects and designers were swept away by the Cotswolds's ideal of craftsmanship and the concept of integrated house and garden. *Country Life in America*, *House and Garden*, *House Beautiful*, and other architectural publications regularly featured the work of British architects. In the early 1900s, when large Beaux-Arts estates were proliferating across the country, a dedicated group of architects and designers began heralding smaller, simpler houses with intimately scaled, naturalistic gardens. Built with indigenous materials with regional variations, these houses and their ancillary garden structure embraced the Arts and Crafts Movement's aesthetic of rusticity and the vernacular.

The American Arts and Crafts Movement reflected the country's melting pot of nationalities and its diverse geography, typically developing symbiotic relationships with firmly established regional traditions. In the Northeast, it attached itself to the deeply entrenched Colonial Revival Movement, which harked back to colonial America, with clapboard houses and romantic, old-fashioned gardens and quaint garden furnishings. In the Midwest, it was linked to the Prairie School, notably in

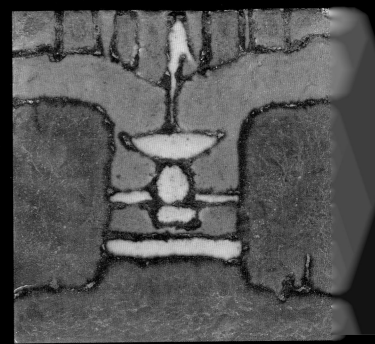

the work of Frank Lloyd Wright and his followers, and landscape architects Jens Jensen and Ossian Cole Simonds, who embraced Robinson's call for wild gardening with native plants.[1] In California, where the Bungalow style reigned as the ideal Arts and Crafts home, naturalistic gardens with native plants were more appropriate than formal ones.

While these are only broad generalizations, the movement was dissipated, and few houses

Dard Hunter, *The Peristyle of the Roycroft Inn, East Aurora, New York* (The Roycrofter, January 1928). Author's Collection

Arts and Crafts Movement had a greater impact on architecture and its allied arts than it did on garden design, where its influence surfaces in details rather than overall concept. In Boston, Chicago, New York, and California, the primary hubs of the movement, Arts and Crafts communities sprang up to carry on Morris's call for artistic reform and joy in manual work. As a result, the American Arts and Crafts Movement has come to be identified with simple oak furniture, decorative pottery and tiles, textiles, book arts, and metalwork, as well as distinctive regional architecture. One of the realms in which the American movement outshone its British mentors was in art pottery, where Rookwood, Grueby, Newcomb, Paul Revere, Batchelder, and other legendary potteries specialized in soft, subtle glazes and simplified floral and landscape motifs. On the other end of the spectrum, Tiffany Studios became synonymous with dazzling, three-dimensional stained-glass panels and lampshades decorated with wisteria, irises, and other flowers in heavenly garden settings.

In 1906, an American writer observed that the Arts and Crafts Movement "had been necessarily somewhat slow in this country, as many have opposed its teachings. However, the strong personality of a few craftsmen has, by protest and example, shown the value of beauty of form and finish."[2] One of those strong personalities was Elbert Hubbard (1856–1915), whose Roycroft community in East Aurora, New York, was founded in direct response to William Morris's example. A former soap salesman, Hubbard realized his dream to found a craft enterprise on the premise that "life without industry is guilt—industry without art is brutality." From 1895 on, the renowned Roycroft Press produced publications ranging from utilitarian tracts such as *The Philistine* and *Little Journeys* to hand-printed volumes illustrated by the famed book designer Dard Hunter. In its heyday, Hubbard employed over two hundred artisans, or Roycrofters, who produced hand-hammered metalwork, books, and furniture in the Roycroft Shops that were sold nationwide. After Hubbard's death in the sinking of the *Lusitania*, Roycroft was taken over by his son, but foundered shortly thereafter when the appeal of such products had greatly diminished.

Gustav Stickley (1858–1942), often regarded as the American William Morris, had an overwhelming influence on middle-class American homeowners through *The Craftsman* magazine, which reached households from coast to coast between 1901 and 1916, the peak years of the American Arts and Crafts Movement. *The Craftsman* extolled the work of English architects and helped translate their ideas into an American Craftsman style. Stickley also offered a line of Craftsman Homes, or inexpensive model bungalows, with regional variations from California Mission style to a mountain camp or a half-timbered cement cottage. A furniture maker, metal worker, and stone mason himself, Stickley founded a furniture workshop in Syracuse, New York, after meeting C.F.A. Voysey and C. R. Ashbee in England in 1898. Like many American artisans and architects, he subscribed to *The International Studio*, which acquainted him with Voysey, Baillie Scott, and Ashbee, whose Guild of Handicraft became a personal inspiration for him.

The Craftsman, April 1911. Author's Collection

M.H. Baillie Scott,
*House at Short Hills, New
Jersey* (from *Studio Yearbook
of Decorative Art,* 1914).
Author's Collection

In 1908 Stickley embarked on Craftsman Farms, a coopera-
tive communal venture located in northern New Jersey, join-
ing the ranks of "American artists, reformers, writers, and
architects who were seeking to remake the world," according
to his biographer Mark Alan Hewitt.[3] Stickley's utopian community embodied many of the ideals of the American Arts and
Crafts Movement—in particular the virtues of the simple life,
manual labor in crafts, and the nurturing of the unspoiled
rural countryside—but went bankrupt in 1915. It was here that
he manufactured his distinctive oak furniture for sale in showrooms in New York City. Stickley constructed a rustic cabin at
Craftsman Farms from chestnut logs gathered on the property, with a clay tile roof and a huge stone chimney. The living
room, which one writer dubbed "nobly barbaric" for its massive rough-hewn posts, was furnished with products made in
the workshops, and the color scheme ran to somber browns,
greens, and gold.[4] Naturalistically planted evergreens and bar-

berry blended harmoniously with the rustic cabin in its rural hillside setting, and vineyards, peach and apple orchards, beds filled with gaily colored cosmos and petunias, and vegetable gardens provided a sense of self-sufficiency.

The pages of *The Craftsman* promoted the natural garden as opposed to what Stickley termed "the rich man's garden, ostentatious, spectacular, sumptuous." The house should be set in the midst of the garden.

> *Let garden and house float together in one harmonious whole, the one finding completion in the other. . . . A garden must be spontaneous—allowed to spring from the ground in a natural way—otherwise it is devoid of that irresistible something called style, for style is born of the shaping of use and beauty to environment. . . . Let your garden look as if it had grown of its own accord, as if Nature herself had been your architect, your landscape gardener, your designer in chief.*[6]

In an ideal garden, no one should be able to tell where the house ends and the garden begins. Pergolas, he advised, were an ideal connection between house and the healthful outdoors; they served to gracefully screen unattractive buildings, lead from one area to the next, and provide outdoor living spaces and pleasant retreats. Stickley's advice was far-ranging in defining the craftsman style of gardens.

Not far from Craftsman Farms, Baillie Scott designed The Close, a half-timbered courtyard house in Short Hills, New Jersey, in 1912.[7] A well-heeled community within commuting distance to New York City, in the 1910s and 1920s Short Hills thrived on sumptuous houses and gardens that Stickley would have dismissed as the "rich man's garden." The client, Henry Binsse, had spotted the article about Runton Old Hall in *House Beautiful* in 1911 and decided he wanted something of an old English inn for his own house.[8] It could not have been more different from Craftsman Farms, with its faint rose-colored stucco façade, half-timbering, leaded-glass casement windows, and decorative lead rainwater heads. The Close is enclosed by low stucco walls, with a garden house next to the gated entry drive. The interior courtyard has simple flower borders, with a more formal treatment at the main entrance; elaborate English-style flower gardens once stood to one side of the house.

Chicago was an unusually fertile area for the American Arts and Crafts Movement. Not only was it home to the Prairie School of architecture, but also the prestigious architectural publication, *House Beautiful*, whose first issue in 1896 featured the work of Voysey and Ashbee. The Chicago Arts and Crafts Society, one of the oldest in the country, was established in 1897 at Jane Addams's Hull House. Frank Lloyd Wright, who was among the charter members, delivered his famous lecture, "The Art and Craft of the Machine," there in 1901. The society's annual exhibitions of members' work fueled many industries, such as pottery, textiles, bookbinding, jewelry, and metalwork. Ashbee's link to Chicago began in 1898, when some of his jewelry was exhibited in one of the society's exhibitions, and he personally came to Chicago two years later, the first of several trips to America.[9]

Chicago was especially renowned for its architecture, which dramatically shifted in focus from Beaux-Arts, as exemplified at the World's Columbian Exposition in 1893, to a new agenda as devised by Frank Lloyd Wright (1867–1959), whose organic approach to design revolutionized the American home. Wright, who was unusually verbose about his personal life and architectural goals, was in many ways a disciple of William Morris. He sought harmony between architecture and the natural landscape and even recommended Gertrude Jekyll's book *Home and Garden* for its special approach to home-building ("It should be in every library.")[10] Evocative renderings by Marion Mahoney Griffin of his early houses include lush, stylized landscapes, with swags of wisteria framing the all-important views to his buildings. Wright-designed planters overflow with trailing vines that accentuate the long, low lines of his Prairie style houses, such as the 1908 Robie House in Chicago. His compounds at Taliesin in Spring Green, Wisconsin, and Taliesin West in the Arizona desert were founded on principles deriving from the Arts and Crafts Movement.

Other, less famous Chicago architects were also influenced by the Arts and Crafts Movement. Howard Van Doren Shaw (1869–1926), who designed country houses in Lake Forest and other fashionable suburbs ringing Chicago, was a devoted Anglophile and conversant with his British contemporaries. Ragdale, Shaw's summer house and country retreat for his growing family, is located in a once-rural farm property with an old apple orchard and views to acres of meadows. Today it is hailed as "one of the finest examples of Arts and Crafts architecture in America, because it has remained untouched and is well preserved."[11] The twin-gabled white stucco house with low, swooping roofs and wood shutters with heart motifs, bears a striking resemblance to Voysey's own house, The Orchard, built the following year. The interior is unpainted oak, with light, airy rooms, inglenooks, and fireplaces; the dining room was once papered with one of Voysey's patterns. Porches around the house link it with the gardens and the distant meadows.

Howard Van Doren Shaw,
Ragdale, Lake Forest, Illinois,
2003

Dovecote in flower garden at
Ragdale, 2003

In comparison with Shaw's more classically inspired gardens, Ragdale is more homespun and personal. Over the years he and his family enhanced the grounds with kitchen and vegetable gardens, flower gardens, a bowling green, and an outdoor theatre, known as the Ragdale Ring, where audiences watched performances by his wife, Frances Wells Shaw.[12] The pleasant flower garden has cross-axial paths, a flourishing grape arbor, a wellhead, and an English-inspired dovecote at one end. At the center of the garden enclosure, a sundial, designed by Shaw himself, is inscribed "Hours Fly. Flowers Die. New Ways. New Days. Pass By. Love Stays." Shaw's garden-planning at Ragdale fits within the parameters laid down by William Morris and William Robinson, with its essential combination of work and leisure and its harmonious link with nature, where informal lanes rambled through the woods to the meadows beyond.[13]

In California, the American Arts and Crafts Movement found its greatest fulfillment. The land of golden opportunity, California is renowned for its delightful climate and the promise of healthful living. Wealthy industrialists looking for vacation homes and artists alike were attracted to the sweeping views of mountains, the sparkling sunshine, and fresh air that were in short supply in Chicago, Boston, and New York. The climate varied considerably, from hot and desert-like in the south to cool and moist in the San Francisco Bay Area. In architecture, the Spanish influence prevailed, with its indigenous adobe Mission architecture, coupled with the outdoor lifestyle brought by Mexican settlers. Mission Revival houses and gardens were to California what the Colonial Revival was to the Northeast. Gardens were ideally suited to the West Coast, where the Mediterranean climate lends itself to outdoor living, with terraces and courtyards. Walled enclosures hugging the house range from a simple courtyard to a series of garden rooms, each with a different theme. The English influence was not a strong consideration in California, where gardens tended to be informal. Californians also had a special bond with nature and a wonderful palette of plants both native and imported.

California also had its fair share of visionaries, such as Charles Fletcher Lummis, whose passion for California missions and Spanish culture in general led him to build an extraordinary house in Pasadena in 1898. Built from round boulders collected from the Arroyo Seco, El Alisal (The Place of Sycamores) overlooked a true Robinsonian wildflower meadow. In that same year in Berkeley, the poet Charles Augustus Keeler formed the Hillside Club, an improvement society aimed at transforming the Berkeley hills into a lush, naturalistic landscape. Keeler teamed up with architect Bernard R. Maybeck (1862–1957) to build his own house, which he hoped his neighbors would emulate. Keeler's book, *The Simple Home* (1904) became somewhat of a bible for his ideas regarding housing reform. About gardens, he wrote: "My own preference for a garden for the simple home is a compromise between the natural and formal types—a compromise in which the carefully studied plan is concealed by a touch of careless grace that makes it appear as if nature had unconsciously made bowers and paths and sheltering hedges."[14] Maybeck was known for his highly original structures in the San Francisco Bay Area, especially in Berkeley, built from local materials. His hallmark wisteria-covered trellises merge imperceptibly with the timber buildings.

California's distinctive architecture was formulated around the California bungalow, which lent itself to porches, terraces, and outdoor spaces. A number of architects left their mark on the California landscape, but none more so than Charles Sumner Greene (1868–1957) and his brother Henry Mather Greene (1870–1954). In many ways, they were comparable to the Barnsley brothers in England, as they were both architects and woodworkers. Born in Ohio and educated in manual arts in St. Louis, they studied architecture at the Massachusetts Institute of Technology in Cambridge, Massachusetts, and later apprenticed with Boston architects. Upon opening their first office in Pasadena in 1894, they created some of the most brilliant examples of Arts and Crafts architecture in the

Charles Greene, Green Gables, Woodside, California, 2002

Charles Greene, Water garden at Green Gables, Woodside, California, 2002

country, demonstrating their exquisite workmanship, detailing, and planning. Rejecting the prevailing Beaux-Arts approach to design, they were particularly influenced by the simplicity of Japanese architecture and furniture.[15]

Charles Sumner Greene traveled to Britain in 1901, where he was exposed to the Arts and Crafts Movement, visiting, among other places, the Glasgow International Exhibition where Mackintosh's work was displayed. Regular subscribers to *The Craftsman*, the brothers began designing furnishings for their architectural commissions in 1904. After visiting Charles' workshops in 1909, C. R. Ashbee wrote: "I think C. Sumner Greene's work beautiful; among the best there is in this country. . . beautiful cabinets and chairs [executed with] a supreme feeling for the material, quite up to our best English craftsmanship."[16]

The David B. Gamble House in Pasadena, designed in 1908, is legendary for its exquisite detailing both inside and out, its sensitive grading, and Japanese-inspired landscaping. As Henry recalled, "we were able to do our best design when we could control a complete landscape and then decorate it, as well as the house. This is the only possible way to achieve integration of all three."[17] The terraces, which function as outdoor living spaces, hug the low, cantilevered house on three sides, under a canopy of California live oaks (*Quercus agrifolia*). Live oaks figure in Charles's magnificent teak-framed front door with its iridescent glass panels that were executed by local craftsmen. The interior is fully furnished with Greene and Greene furniture, paneling, and lighting fixtures. The Blacker House, designed in 1907 and also located

Charles Greene, Rustic stone grotto at Green Gables, 2002

in Pasadena, is noted for its Japanese-inspired garden that melds beautifully with the architecture. Charles commented, "fine gardens are like fine pictures, only it may take longer to paint them with nature's brush."[18]

Green Gables in Woodside is Charles Sumner Greene's masterpiece of landscape architecture. Designed for Mortimer Fleishhacker in 1911, the long, low house is sited in the midst of seventy-five acres of rolling meadows dotted with live oaks and views to the Santa Cruz Mountains. Charles, who envisioned the garden as living rooms for the house, created a series of terraces and reflecting pools to capitalize on the expansive view to the distant mountains. In 1926 he designed a spectacular water garden in a problematic area where the site dropped off dramatically. His brilliant three-hundred-foot-long pool terminates in a series of stone arches reminiscent of a Roman aqueduct. The garden, in fact, quotes many sites in Italy, England, and America. Looking back to the house from the lower garden, one sees a rustic stone grotto nestled between the massive horseshoe staircases ascending to the upper terrace. The lower garden is constructed in a warm-toned stone in a vernacular style of craftsmanship. The skillful planting of native and imported plants with strong architectural interest complements the rustic stonework in the staircases and paths. David C. Streatfield, the preeminent scholar of California gardens, believes that Green Gables is the largest garden in the country by an Arts and Crafts designer.[19] It is certainly one of the most significant and remains unchanged today.

Chapter 12 | Beautiful Gardens in America.

In her 1915 book, *Beautiful Gardens in America*, Louise Shelton asked: "Just as there are gardens peculiar to other nations. . . . might we not give serious consideration to evolving someday a type particularly American [that embodies] the poetic and artistic sense of our country?"[1] For the same reasons that the American Arts and Crafts Movement was regional, there could never be a national garden style due to too many differences in climate, plant palette, and heritage. In the Northeast, the tradition of old-fashioned American gardens, based to some extent on those of the early English settlers, was deeply entrenched. These gardens were companionable with eighteenth-century houses as well as new houses built along traditional lines. Sometimes called grandmother's gardens, they were captured on canvas by many well-known American Impressionist artists.[2] Historian and antiquarian Alice Morse Earle was one of the first to recognize these uniquely American gardens. Her books, such as *Old-Time Gardens Newly Set Forth* (1901) and *Sun-Dials and Roses of Yesterday* (1902), present a nostalgic view of the colonial era embodied by the Colonial Revival. The Colonial Revival Movement, which focused on architecture and interior design, was a pervasive element in American cultural history, embracing an idealized view of the nation's past. In some respects, it was a reaction to nineteenth-century industrialization, the same force that galvanized Morris into action decades earlier in England.

Colonial Revival gardens are characterized by their straightforward geometric configuration, linear pathways, architectural features such as arbors, and fences for enclosure. Billowing flower borders edged with boxwood, fragrant shrubs and vines, and fruit trees were memorable elements. The key to these gardens was their domestic scale and simplicity, which was the dominant aesthetic of gardens designed by homeowners in the Northeast. Landscape architects were more likely to respond to European Beaux-Arts and Italianate sensibilities in grander estates.

The rediscovery of America's past in the Northeast came with an explosion of interest in gardening and a proliferation of popular books aimed at a largely female audience. Written mostly by New Englanders, books such as Helena Rutherfurd Ely's *A Woman's Hardy Garden* (1903) and Mable Osgood Wright's *The Garden You and I* (1906), reached out to women who sought not only a

Augustus Saint-Gaudens, *Flower gardens at Saint-Gaudens National Historic Site, Cornish, New Hampshire, 2002*

pastime, but an outlet for their creative energy. They addressed not only the practical side of gardening, but its therapeutic rewards as well.[3] Most of the women who read these books managed households smaller than the large Victorian estates of the mid-nineteenth century manned by teams of gardeners.

In 1893 the highly respected architectural critic Mariana Griswold Van Rensselaer brought aristocratic recognition to gardening arts with her book, *Art Out-of-Doors: Hints on Good Taste on Gardening*, which argued for consideration of gardening as an art. She defined the landscape gardener as "a gardener, an engineer, and an artist, who like an architect considers beauty and utility together."[4] This idea spurred a new field for women as garden designers and eventually landscape architects, a profession in which Beatrix Farrand, Ellen Shipman, and others became leaders in the early 1900s. As opposed to the male-dominated firms that specialized in parks and large estates, women found their own niche designing small residential gardens distinguished by sophisticated plantings and architectural features inspired by the Arts and Crafts Movement.[5]

In addition to Roycroft and Craftsman Farms, the East Coast flourished with other Arts and Crafts communities, such as the Byrdcliffe Colony in Woodstock, New York, and Rose Valley in Pennsylvania. The Cornish Colony in New Hampshire, however, was renowned for its gardens as well as its resident artists. Located in an area of exceptional natural beauty on the banks of the Connecticut River and overlooking Mount Ascutney in Vermont, the colony centered around the renowned American Renaissance sculptor Augustus Saint-Gaudens (1843–1907), who arrived in 1885, seeking relief from the summer heat of his New York City studio. His garden melded the Colonial Revival aesthetic in its configuration and plantings with pergolas, benches, and other classically inspired ornament. Saint-Gaudens in turn attracted other artists, such as Charles Platt, Thomas Dewing, and Stephen Parrish, who all created trend-setting gardens. In 1906, one critic declared that Cornish enjoyed the distinction of being "the most beautifully gardened village in all America."[6]

No one did more to mold the Cornish style of gardening than Charles Adams Platt (1861–1933), an etcher and landscape painter who later turned to garden design and architecture, building nearly a dozen significant houses in the colony.[7] Platt developed an architectural style that always ensured the cosy relationship of house and garden with brick terraces and indoor-outdoor areas, such as loggias that framed the views out. His axial gardens, screened by masses of shrubbery to control these all-important views, were filled with luxu-

Charles A. Platt (1861–1933), *Larkspur* (at High Court), oil on canvas, 1895. Courtesy members of the Platt family

Stephen Parrish (1846–1938), *Garden Staircase* (at Northcote), oil on canvas, c. 1907. Private Collection

rious flower gardens. Platt's protégées Ellen Shipman and Rose Standish Nichols, both Cornish neighbors whom he tutored in design, carried on his work in a special style of gardening.

The garden of Stephen Parrish (1846–1938) was the pinnacle of Cornish gardening, from its overall conception to its skillful planting. Located on the side of an exposed hillside, where gardening was especially challenging, Parrish's Northcote exemplifies the true mingling of house and garden. A landscape painter, and the father of Maxfield Parrish (who illustrated Edith Wharton's book, *Italian Villas and Their Gardens*), Parrish nestled his picturesque flower garden into the L-shaped house, designed by the Philadelphia architect Wilson Eyre. It was further sheltered by arbors festooned with wild grapes and Virginia creeper. In midsummer the garden

was filled with hollyhocks, lilies, hardy phlox, and poppies, all stalwarts of traditional New England gardens. The tradition of Cornish gardening lives on in small residential gardens that capitalize on the historic tradition and the breathtaking views of the countryside.

Around the same time, a small summer colony flourished on Eastern Point, in Gloucester, Massachusetts, centered around a loosely-knit group of antiquarians, connoisseurs, decorators, and artists. The circle included the renowned portrait painter Cecilia Beaux, Harvard professor Abram Piatt Andrew, Philadelphia arts patron Caroline Sinkler, and others, including their mutual friend Isabella Stewart Gardner.[8] The person who left the most significant mark was Henry Davis Sleeper (1878–1934), an interior designer who created

Beauport as a showcase for his extensive collections of antiques. Sleeper's highly individualistic sense of style can be found in both house and grounds that reflect his cosmopolitan, yet homespun approach to design. As his collections grew, Sleeper transformed a pleasant shingle style house into a fanciful, ecclectic dwelling burgeoning with period rooms.

The gardens, a series of outdoor rooms encircling the house, exemplify both the Colonial Revival and the compartmentalized English formal garden as explicated in Blomfield's book. Rustic stone terraces and arbors, sundials, and collections of garden ornament reflect Arts and Crafts sensibilities in their layout and execution, while the plantings of each of the areas are a response to the Colonial Revival aesthetic. Hollyhocks in deep tones of maroon and chocolatey-brown

that he favored in his interiors provide a striking note against the fieldstone terrace embedded with grass.

The English overlay in East Coast gardens was a strong factor. English-inspired knot gardens, geometrically hedged green gardens, and perennial borders went well with Tudor Revival houses that proliferated in America in the 1920s. The intricate Elizabethan-style knot garden at Thornedale, in Millbrook, New York, designed by landscape architect Nellie B. Allen (1869–1960) in 1934 for Mrs. Oakleigh Thorne reflects the designer's reverence for English gardens. A devotée of Gertrude Jekyll, Allen was a frequent visitor to Munstead Wood and other English gardens, such as Great Dixter's famed topiary gardens.[9] Ladew Topiary Gardens, Monkton, Maryland, are one of the most extravagant topiary

gardens in America. Created by Harvey Ladew in the late 1920s, the expansive gardens are an ode to fox hunting in the heart of Maryland hunt country. Fanciful hounds and birds, as well as billowing hedges trimmed as garlands or sculpted obelisks astonish visitors. Ladew was a devoted Anglophile, who regularly visited the great houses and gardens as well as attended hunts all over England, enjoying friendships with the Duke and Duchess of Windsor, among others.

Rose Standish Nichols (1872–1960), a Boston landscape architect and the niece of Saint-Gaudens, specialized in flower gardens and often collaborated with Howard Van Doren Shaw and David Adler in Lake Forest. Nichols toured England and studied briefly with F. Inigo Thomas as well as Platt in Cornish. In 1902, her book, *English Pleasure Gardens*, revealed the depth

Opposite:
Isabella Stewart Gardner in Caroline Sinkler's Garden, Gloucester, Massachusetts, c. 1915. Courtesy A. Piatt Andrew Archive

Above:
Nellie B. Allen's *knot garden at Thornedale, Millbrook, New York, 1934. Author's Collection*

Left:
Henry Davis Sleeper, *Front entrance to Beauport, Gloucester, Massachusetts, 1910. Courtesy Society for the Preservation of New England Antiquities*

Ladew Topiary Gardens, Monkton, Maryland, 1990

of her knowledge of English garden history and her unfailing critical eye as a designer. Writing about Gertrude Jekyll's garden, for example, she comments, "It is seldom that both wild and cultivated flowers have been grouped more successfully."[10] Pen and ink drawings that she supplied for her book are executed in the style of Thomas's illustrations for Blomfield's book. Nichols's reverence for the revival of the Elizabethan style, with its walled enclosures, green courts, pavilions, and wealth of flowers, surfaces in her own commissions.[11]

Gertrude Jekyll's books left an indelible mark on American gardeners. As Louise Beebe Wilder, one of America's most important garden writers, wrote, "Miss Jekyll made us believe ourselves artists in embryo with a color box to our hands and a canvas ready stretched before us."[12] As she explained in *Colour in My Garden* (1918), Americans found the practical application of Jekyll's advice difficult to achieve in widely variable climates. Wilder recounts her own trials and occasional minor successes with Jekyll's recommendations in America's shorter, hotter, and drier summers. Flowers bloomed for days, rather than weeks, and the diffused bluish cast to the sky that enhances so many British gardens is more apt to be intensely bright sunlight in American gardens, thus changing the perception of color.

Jekyll's recommended plantings in her three American commissions, which she did not personally visit, were fraught with problems due to her inexperience with the American climate

Herbaceous borders overlooking Lake Champlain at Shelburne Farms, Shelburne, Vermont, 1992

Beatrix Farrand, Garden bench at Dumbarton Oaks, Washington, D.C., 1987

and plant palette.[13] At the Old Glebe House in Woodbury, Connecticut, she designed a cottage-style garden (now restored), with a white picket fence and color-graded borders that were pleasant, but undistinguishable from any number of New England gardens.[14] The renowned horticulturist Henry Francis du Pont, creator of the garden at Winterthur, Delaware, took Jekyll's recommendations to heart. Jottings in his notebooks after visits to Munstead Wood include suggestions for using clematis to create a "pulled-over Jekyll effect behind the Delphiniums" that has baffled gardeners for nearly a century.[15]

Of the many gardens in America that owe some of their inspiration to Robinson and Jekyll's books, Shelburne Farms is one that blends many different themes. Overlooking Lake Champlain in Vermont, Shelburne Farms represents the boundless energies and resources of Lila Vanderbilt Webb (her brother George Vanderbilt established the French-inspired Biltmore Estate in Asheville, North Carolina). She started off with an elaborate Italianate garden, with long pergolas, reflecting pools, and beds of annuals. In 1920, she became smitten with the informal cottage-garden style as popularized by Robinson and Jekyll. Guided by Alice Martineau's book, *The Herbaceous Garden,* she filled her grand allée with herbaceous plants, separated by an English-style, wide turf walk. Masses of achillea, aquilegia, campanulas, coreopsis, hollyhock, lilies, and other perennials, arranged in clusters of hot and cool tones, replaced the Victorian-style potted dracaenas of earlier years.[16]

While *Colour in the Flower Garden* inspired amateur gardeners about plantings, *Gardens for Small Country Houses* opened many eyes to garden architecture and the practical considerations of garden design. It was especially influential on architects and landscape architects, who replicated English-style garden buildings. Beatrix Farrand (1872–1959), who was one of America's foremost landscape architects, executed nearly 200 projects, from small cottage-style gardens to large estate gardens with Beaux-Arts underpinnings to campus planning.[17] Not exclusively a flower garden designer, as were many of her female colleagues, Farrand painted her landscapes with a broader brush. At Dumbarton Oaks, in Washington, D.C., considered her masterpiece, Farrand laid out a series of formal-style garden rooms hugging the house, with Robinson-inspired naturalistic areas on the hilly outer perimeter. An excellent horticulturist, Farrand excelled at naturalistic groupings of native trees and shrubs, as well as intertwining architecture and plants. She also excelled in the design of garden gates, benches, planters, and small buildings that reflect the Arts and Crafts approach to individuality and craftmanship.

Ellen Biddle Shipman (1869–1950) can be considered the greatest proponent of the beautiful American flower garden and the equal of Gertrude Jekyll in her knowledge of horticulture and her artistic approach to the design of small gardens. After training in Cornish with Charles Platt, she went on to become one of the country's most sought-after designers, specializing in small residential gardens, with bountiful plantings and elegant furnishings, all done in a Colonial Revival or rusticated Arts and Crafts mode. Her library was filled with all the key volumes on English garden design, including many of Jekyll's books. Beginning in the mid-1910s, she was among the first to routinely use Lutyens's famous garden bench in her commissions. She also lifted design elements directly from the pages of *Gardens for Small Country Houses*, including Triggs's water rill at Little Boarhunt, which resurfaces in a Massachusetts garden in the 1920s, and his dovecote at Chatham Manor in Virginia. Architectural furnishings, such as dovecotes modeled after English and American examples, are one of the trademarks of her style.

Ellen Biddle Shipman, English-style dovecote in Salvage garden, Glen Head, New York, 1935. Courtesy Division of Rare and Manuscript Collections, Cornell University Library

Above:
Ellen Biddle Shipman,
Water rill at McGinley Garden,
Milton, Massachusetts, 1932.
Courtesy Rare and Manuscript
Collections, Cornell University
Library

Opposite:
Ellen Biddle Shipman, *English*
Garden at Stan Hywet Hall,
Akron, Ohio, 1998

Shipman, who was only an armchair traveler, was thoroughly American in her approach to design and planting, as opposed to many of her colleagues who embraced the Beaux-Arts aesthetic from travel abroad. Throughout her career she relied on the axial Colonial Revival layout, with shaded walks overhung with wisteria and lilac and copious plantings of perennials, flowering shrubs, and ornamental trees. Using this basic vocabulary, she created some of the most elegant, domestically scaled gardens of the era that stand well in comparison with those of her best English counterparts. The English Garden at Stan Hywet Hall, in Akron, Ohio, exemplifies her comfortable approach to design and scale. At the heart of her designs was the intimate relationship of house and garden, which she achieved through enclosure and architectural effects.

As a planting designer, she used bold blocks of color in a stained-glass window effect rather than the impressionistic drifts that were Jekyll's specialty. The secret to her success as a designer lay in limiting herself to no more than six to eight

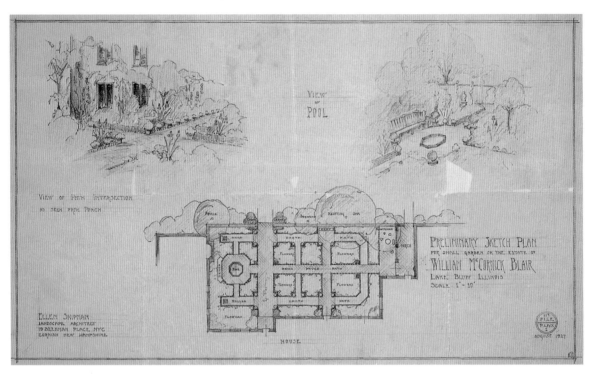

Above:
Ellen Biddle Shipman, *Preliminary Sketch Plan for Small Garden on the Estate of William McCormick Blair,* colored pencil drawing, 1927. Courtesy Mr. and Mrs. John H. Bryan

Opposite:
Walled garden at Crabtree Farm, Lake Bluff, Illinois, 2003

main flowering plants, letting each in season "dominate the garden. For the time one flower is the guest of honor and is merely supplemented with other flowers," she wrote.[18] But, she cautioned, "planting, however beautiful, is not a garden. A garden must be enclosed. . . or otherwise it would merely be a cultivated area."[19] For the essential enclosure she used existing woodlands or planted dense groups of hemlocks or other fast-growing trees to form a backdrop for her perennial borders. Her gardens were more three-dimensional than Jekyll's, with an overhead canopy of flowering trees color-coordinated to complement the borders below. Wisteria-clad pergolas and furnishings, such as benches, statuary, and wooden gates, completed her garden pictures.

Whereas Farrand tended to control all aspects of her design, Shipman gladly collaborated with many of the nation's foremost traditionalist architects, including Platt, with whom she had a decade-long partnership rivaling that of Lutyens and Jekyll. Other architects included the cream of American estate builders, such as David Adler, Delano and Aldrich, Harrie T. Lindeberg, Mott B. Schmidt, John F. Staub, and Horace Trumbauer, as well as Warren Manning and a host of notable landscape architects. At Crabtree Farm, on a bluff north of Chicago overlooking Lake Michigan, Shipman designed a colonial-style garden as a perfect complement to David Adler's summer house for the William McCormick Blair family in 1926. It was a small component of a larger estate, a former dairy farm, surrounded by acres of lush woodlands. Designed so that there were axial views to the woodlands, this tiny formal garden is edged with low, clipped boxwood hedges surrounding beds originally filled with peonies.

Shipman's garden, with intersecting patterned brick paths and a tiny reflecting pool and bench in one corner is in perfect harmony with the house, one of the basic tenets of the Arts and Crafts Movement. Other American designers who embraced the Arts and Crafts Movement endowed their creations with simplicity, a heightened sensitivity to materials, and the essential integration of house and garden.

Epilogue. Many of the characteristics of the Arts and Crafts garden, namely craftsmanship, sophisticated plantsmanship, intimacy of scale, and harmonious relationship with the house, are still relevant for today's smaller gardens. Whether the house is an Edwardian manor or a modest suburban dwelling, gardens can be created that pay their respects to the guiding principles of the Arts and Crafts Movement. It is fitting to conclude with a few examples of contemporary gardens that show how this can be successfully achieved.

Bryan's Ground, near Presteigne in Herefordshire, is a Tuscan-toned half-timbered Edwardian house dating from 1913 that is poised on the banks of the River Lugg on the border between England and Wales. An existing kitchen garden with high brick walls and a thick yew hedge as well as a sunk garden to the south of the house provided the underpinnings for a new garden that continues to grow. Since 1993, Bryan's Ground has been the home of David Wheeler and Simon Dorrell, editor and art director of *Hortus*, a quarterly garden publication founded by Wheeler in 1987. The garden proper occupies two acres, the largest feature being the old kitchen garden that has been divided into quadrants, each with a different focus. A for-

mal garden, canal garden, topiary garden, and other areas have been developed, each named after a significant place or person. St. Anne's (for Anne Raver, the *New York Times* reporter who first wrote about *Hortus*), Standen (Philip Webb's house), the George Walk (a beloved dog's constitutional run), the Orchard Plats (carpeted with *Iris sibirica* in the spring), St. Ives (a timber potting shed), the Lighthouse (a garden folly that was originally a domestic gas plant), the Sulking House, and so on. The newest, and most ambitious undertaking is the Arboretum

Hortus is a publication in the true Arts and Crafts manner. Beautifully designed and produced, with thoughtful typesetting and artists' line drawings for illustrations,

Simon Dorrell, *In the Sunk Garden Bryan's Ground,* ink drawing (*Hortus,* Spring 1994)

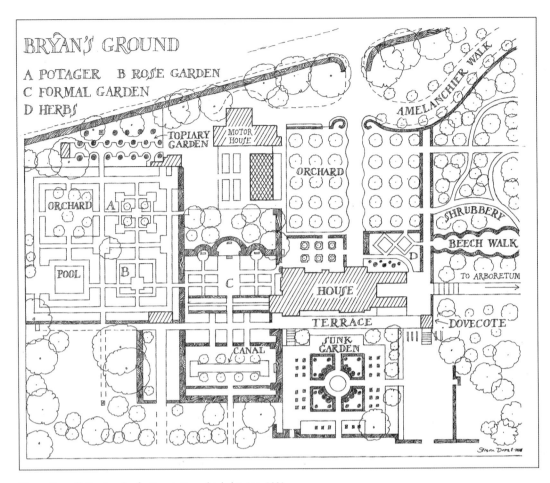

Simon Dorrell, *Garden plan for Bryan's Ground,* ink drawing, 2003

rather than glossy photographs, it features the cream of British (and some American) writers who contribute garden memoirs and literature as well as profiles of interesting designers and gardens. York Gate, in Adel, Yorkshire, which was the subject of a four-part series in *Hortus*, is remarkable for its small scale, ingenious planning, and exquisite detailing. Located in a suburban community five miles from Leeds, the garden comprises less than an acre. It was designed by the Spencer family, beginning in 1951: Frederick Spencer, a surveyor; his wife Sybil, who oversaw the garden until her recent death; and their son Robin, who was also a surveyor. The garden has an ordered geometry in its planting and detailing, but an informality in how the twelve or so compartments interlock imperceptibly with one another, creating both intimacy and the illusion of a far larger place. The planting scheme is architectural, with an emphasis on a diversity of foliage, texture, and form, mostly in shades of green, rather than on a flowery confection. Linear waves of

dark hedges, golden globes of yew, and spikes of evergreens balance water features and simple garden ornaments, such as a row of lead cans, an obelisk, or the rustic paving.

Tony Ridler's minimalist half-acre garden, near Swansea, Wales, is a new undertaking, conceived as a series of defined spaces with an emphasis on hedges of yew, Portugal laurel, and box and tightly manipulated companion plantings of santolina, hostas, hellebores, and other plants with strong foliage interest. The tiny terrace house is nearly engulfed by the long, linear T-shaped garden (composed of several family allotments). Neatly clipped box spheres and spirals of yew are offset by the odd window in a hedge that allows a peek into the next area. Walls painted black and other artful effects reveal Ridler's profession as a graphic designer. Beautifully executed and highly original, Ridler's garden owes little to the self-conscious replicas of iconic gardens that more conventional designers revel in.

Simon Dorrell, York Gate, ink drawing (Hortus, Autumn 1995)

Simon Dorrell, Ridler Garden, ink drawing (Hortus, Winter 2002)

Madoo, Robert Dash's spectacular garden in Sagaponack, Long Island, is a true artist's garden. Brilliant hues, such as the yellow door, the lilac summerhouse, and the blue entry gate reflect the personality of this important American Expressionist painter. Nearly forty years in the making, Madoo (which means "My Dove" in Welsh) is highly personal and devoid of all the much-imitated quotations that bedevil most other new gardens. Garden hats hang on posts, box spheres lounge beneath fastigate gingko trees like bowling balls, and ladder-like fences enclose the gardens. Dash is also a well-versed plantsman, propagating many of the plants himself and using them with an artist's eye. In his book, *Notes From Madoo*, he writes: "Foliant umbrage is silvery and cottony below and lanced, blunted, toothed, or indented; strap, ovate, and round; margined with white and yellow or speckled silver."

Taking a leaf from one of Sedding's pages, none of these gardens replicates an actual Arts and Crafts garden, but each one drinks of their spirit.

Notes

INTRODUCTION

1. See Charlotte Gere and Lesley Hoskins, *The House Beautiful: Oscar Wilde and the Aesthetic Interior* (London: Lund Humphries/Geffrye Museum, 2000).

2. Mark Girouard, *Sweetness and Light: The Queen Anne Movement, 1860–1900* (New Haven: Yale University Press, 1984), explores the ramifications of the style in architecture, interiors, and garden design.

3. Ernest Newton, "Domestic Architecture of To-Day," in Lawrence Weaver, ed., *The House and Its Equipment* (London: Country Life, 1912), 1.

4. Margaret Richardson, *The Craft Architects* (New York: Rizzoli, 1983), 11.

5. Judith B. Tankard and Martin A. Wood, *Gertrude Jekyll at Munstead Wood* (New York: Sagapress, 1996), 68–71.

6. For more on these offices, see Richardson, *The Craft Architects*.

7. Hermann Muthesius, *Das Englische Haus* (Berlin: Wasmuth, 1908–1910), vol. 2, 168. Muthesius's three-volume work, originally published in 1904–05, was translated into English in an abridged volume in 1979.

8. Helen Allingham and Marcus B. Huish, *Happy England* (London: Adam and Charles Black, 1903).

9. Mary Greensted, *The Arts and Crafts Movement in the Cotswolds* (Stroud: Alan Sutton, 1993), 1–2.

10. The founders were Gerald Horsley, William Lethaby, Mervyn Macartney, Ernest Newton, and Edward Prior.

11. Muthesius, *Das Englische Haus*, vol. 1, 218.

CHAPTER 1. GARDENS OLD AND NEW

1. For a detailed discussion of Edwardian garden design and the principal architects, see David Ottewill's *The Edwardian Garden* (New Haven: Yale University Press, 1989).

2. Reginald Blomfield, *The Formal Garden in England* (London: Macmillan, 1892), x.

3. Muthesius, *Das Englische Haus*, vol. 1, 218.

4. Newton, "Domestic Architecture of To-Day," 1.

5. The other partners in Kenton and Company (1890–92) were Sidney Barnsley, Ernest Gimson, William Lethaby, and Mervyn Macartney, all from Shaw's office.

6. George S. Elgood and Gertrude Jekyll, *Some English Gardens* (London: Longmans, Green, 1904), 56.

7. For the career of F. Inigo Thomas, see Ottewill, *The Edwardian Garden*, 13–21.

8. Robert Nathan Cram, "Athelhampton Hall," *House Beautiful*, June 1926, 789. In the 1920s, landscape architect Thomas Mawson made further improvements to Athelhampton.

9. John D. Sedding, *Garden-Craft Old and New* (London: John Lane, 1891), vi–vii.

10. Walter Crane, *A Floral Fantasy in an Old English Garden Set Forth in Verses of Coloured Designs by Walter Crane* (London: Harpers, 1899).

11. "A Garden in Westmoreland," *Gardening Illustrated*, 22 November 1884, 459.

12. Elgood and Jekyll, *Some English Gardens*, 63.

13. In 1914, Walter Hindes Godfrey (1881–1961), a former pupil of Devey's architectural partner, wrote a modest book that served to reintroduce Devey nearly thirty years after his death. Ignoring the great strides in garden design that had transpired since the publication of Sedding and Blomfield's books, *Gardens in the Making* continued to champion their basic tenets.

14. Elgood and Jekyll, *Some English Gardens*, 87–89.

15. Elgood and Jekyll, *Some English Gardens*, 24.

16. Muthesius, *Das Englische Haus*, vol. 1, 217.

17. William Robinson, *Garden Design and Architects' Gardens* (London: John Murray, 1892), ix–xi.

18. Robinson, *Garden Design and Architects' Gardens*, 66.

19. Muthesius, *Das Englische Haus*, vol. 1, 218.

CHAPTER 2. WILLIAM MORRIS'S EARTHLY PARADISE

1. J. W. Mackail, *The Life of William Morris* (1899) (New York: Benjamin Blom, 1968), vol. 1, 143.

2. For an excellent discussion of Morris's flowers and gardening interests, see Derek W. Baker, *The Flowers of William Morris* (London: Barn Elms, 1996) and Jill Hamilton, Penny Hart, and John Simmons, *The Gardens of William Morris* (New York: Stewart, Tabori and Chang, 1998).

3. The founders were William Morris, Edward Burne-Jones, Philip Webb, Dante Gabriel Rossetti, Ford Madox Brown, Charles Faulkner, and Peter Paul Marshall. In 1875, Morris reorganized the firm, naming it Morris and Company, and in 1881 he moved it from London to Merton Abbey.

4. May Morris, ed., *The Collected Works of William Morris* (London: Longmans, Green, 1910–15), vol. 22, 77.

5. Examples of the firm's furnishings can be seen at Standen, Wightwick Manor, and Red House, all National Trust properties. Additionally, The William Morris Gallery, Kelmscott Manor, and Victoria and Albert Museum have collections of the firm's work.

6. William Morris, letter to Emma Lazarus, 21 April 1884, in "A Day in Surrey with William Morris," *Century* 32 (July 1886), 397. Emma Lazarus (1849–1887) was a social reformer and poet

whose poem, "The New Colossus," appears on the base of the Statue of Liberty in New York harbor. Lazarus visited Merton Abbey in 1886.

7. William Morris, "Making the Best of It," *Hopes and Fears for Art* (London: Longmans, Green, 1908), 124–25. This was originally given as a paper for the Birmingham Society of Artists in 1879.

8. Morris, *Hopes and Fears for Art*, 126–27.

9. Morris, *Hopes and Fears for Art*, 128.

10. Mackail, *The Life of William Morris*, 143–44.

11. Fiona MacCarthy, *William Morris: A Life for Our Time* (New York: Alfred A. Knopf, 1995), 164.

12. May Morris, *William Morris: Artist, Writer, Socialist* (1936) (New York: Russell and Russell, 1966), vol. 1, 12.

13. The account, possibly by Georgiana Burne-Jones, appears in Aymer Vallance, *William Morris: His Art, His Writings, and His Public Life* (London: George Bell and Sons, 1897), 49.

14. Hermann Muthesius, *The English House* (abridged version of *Das Englische Haus*, 1904–05; New York: Rizzoli, 1979), 17–18; MacCarthy, *William Morris: A Life*, 144.

15. Mackail, *The Life of William Morris*, 144.

16. Jill Hamilton, in "Morris's Garden of Inspiration," *Country Life* 196 (19 September 2002), 166–69, suggests that the lavish plantings were at variance with the austerity of the interior and the symmetry of the garden contrasts with the irregularity of the house.

17. Some of Webb's drawings for Red House (now housed at the Victoria and Albert Museum) are reproduced in Edward Hollamby, *Red House* (New York: Van Nostrand Reinhold, 1991).

18. For a detailed history of the house, see Corona More, "Kelmscott Manor, Oxfordshire: The Home of William Morris," *Country Life* 50 (20 August 1921), 224–29; 27 August 1921, 256–62.

19. After Morris's death in 1896, his widow Jane bought the lease in 1913 and lived there until her death in 1938. After May Morris's death, the house was acquired by the Society of Antiquaries in 1962.

20. William Morris, "Gossip About an Old House on the Upper Thames," *The Quest* (Birmingham Guild of Handicraft), November 1895.

21. Morris, "Gossip about an Old House."

22. Rossetti, letter to his mother, 1871, cited in Vallance, *William Morris*, 191.

23. William Morris, *News from Nowhere* (1891) (London: Longmans, Green, 1910), 264–65.

24. Morris, "Gossip about an Old House."

25. Lazarus, "A Day in Surrey," 394.

CHAPTER 3. THE LURE OF THE COTSWOLDS

1. Norman Jewson, *By Chance I Did Rove*, 2nd ed. (Warwick: privately printed, 1973), 26.

2. W. R. Lethaby, Alfred H. Powell, and F. L. Griggs, *Ernest Gimson: His Life and Work* (Stratford-upon-Avon: Shakespeare Head Press, 1924), 7.

3. Robert Weir Schultz (1860–1951), who worked in the offices of Norman Shaw and later George and Peto, where he overlapped Edwin Lutyens, designed in the vernacular style, but was also fascinated with Byzantine architecture.

4. Liberty and Company, the popular shop on Regent's Street, London, was founded in 1895 by Arthur Lasenby Liberty, who commissioned decorative arts (especially metalwork and textiles) from all the leading designers of the day.

5. The Cheltenham Museum has an extensive collection of their work, including drawings for executed and unexecuted architectural projects.

6. H. Avray Tipping, "Daneway House, Gloucestershire," *Country Life* 25 (6 March 1909), 347.

7. H. Avray Tipping, "Pinbury, Gloucestershire," *Country Life* 27 (30 April 1910), 634–36.

8. H. Avray Tipping, "A House at Sapperton by Mr. A. Ernest Barnsley," *Country Life* 25 (10 April 1909), 522–27. The house, gardens, and stable cost £1,700, proof that careful architectural alterations can cost more than building from scratch.

9. Lethaby et al., *Ernest Gimson: His Life and Work*, 9.

10. H. Avray Tipping, "A House at Sapperton Designed by Mr. Ernest Gimson," *Country Life* 25 (6 March 1909), 348–54. The thatch roof burned in 1941.

11. Gertrude Jekyll and Lawrence Weaver, *Gardens for Small Country Houses* (London: Country Life, 1912), 165–66. Stoneywell Cottage, which Gimson built as a rural retreat for his brother Sydney in 1898, was nestled in among the rough boulders on the site. Gimson's superb placement of the cottage in the natural landscape is an excellent example of the "organic" approach to architecture that many other architects failed miserably at. See Mary Comino, *Gimson and the Barnsleys* (New York: Van Nostrand Reinhold, 1982), 138–39.

12. Tankard and Wood, *Gertrude Jekyll at Munstead Wood*, 135–36.

13. Planting plans and correspondence for Combend Manor are included in the Jekyll Collection, Environmental Design Archives, University of California, Berkeley.

14. For a detailed discussion of the plantings, see David Wheeler and Simon Dorrell, *Over the Hills from Broadway: Images of Cotswold Gardens* (Stroud: Alan Sutton, 1991), 111–116.

15. Jewson, *By Chance I Did Rove*, 13–14.

16. Today Owlpen Manor is a small hotel and furnished with many pieces designed and created in the Sapperton workshops.

17. James Lees-Milne, *Some Cotswold Country Houses* (Stanbridge: Dovecote Press, 1987), 119.

18. Jekyll and Weaver, *Gardens for Small Country Houses*, 2nd ed (1913), xix.

19. Harold D. Eberlein, "Owlpen Manor House, Gloucestershire," *Architectural Forum*, August 1927, 192.

20. An enigmatic figure, Milne went on to great acclaim for his artful house and garden at Coleton Fishacre, in Devon, for Rupert D'Oyly Carte in 1925. See Christopher Hussey, "A Modern Country House, Coleton Fishacre, Devonshire," *Country Life* 67 [31 May 1930], 782–89.

21. Lawrence Weaver, *Small Country Houses of To-Day*, vol. 2 (London: Country Life, 1919), 76. Drakestone House, still owned by the same family, offers bed and breakfast.

22. C. R. Ashbee, journal entry, 1914, as cited in Simon Biddulph, *Rodmarton Manor* (Gloucestershire, privately printed, 2001), 5.

23. Ernest Barnsley worked on Rodmarton from 1909 until his death in January 1926 (with a suspension between 1914 and 1917 due to the First World War), when the project was taken over by his brother Sidney until his death later that year. Rodmarton was completed by Norman Jewson in 1929.

24. Illustrations from 1931 show the Portuguese laurels and other developed parts of the garden. See Arthur Oswald, "Rodmarton, Gloucestershire," *Country Life* 69 (4 April 1931), 422–27.

CHAPTER 4. ARCHITECTURAL GARDENING

1. Charles Holme (1848–1923) lived at Red House from 1876 until 1902, when he purchased the Manor House at Upton Grey in Hampshire (see Chapter 10).

2. Its content was "tailored to the preferences and tastes of the middle-class art lover and amateur [who avoided] the stale academicism of the Royal Academy and its aging mentors," according to Clive Ashwin, " High Art and Low Life: *The Studio* and the *Fin de Siècle*," *Studio International Special Centenary Number*, 1993, 7.

3. Holme's editorial team included editor Gleeson White (who wrote many of the early articles) and art editor C. Lewis Hind (the author of numerous monographs on artists). When Holme retired in 1919, he was succeeded by his son Geoffrey Holme, a brilliant businessman to whom credit should be given for the longevity of the magazine. See *The Studio: A Bibliography, the First Fifty Years, 1893–1943* (London: Sims and Reed, 1978) for a detailed history of the magazine.

4. Bryan Holme, "Introduction," *The Studio: A Bibliography, the First Fifty Years*, 1.

5. William Henry Ward (1865–1924) was a protégé of architect Arthur Blomfield (the uncle of Reginald Blomfield) and the author of two books on French architecture of the Renaissance period. He worked for the firms of George and Peto, Dan Gibson, and Edwin Lutyens.

6. Weaver, in *Small Country Houses of To-Day*, 71–75, praised High Moss as a success, but failed to mention the garden.

7. Hermann Muthesius, *The English House*, 51.

8. Gleeson White, "Some Glasgow Designers," *The Studio* 11 (July 1897), 86–100.

9. Muthesius suggests that their work was initially ridiculed in England, but modern scholarship has begun to dispute this notion.

10. Mackintosh's watercolors are held at the Hunterian Art Gallery, University of Glasgow. See Roger Billcliffe, *Mackintosh Watercolours* (London: John Murray, 1978) and *Architectural Sketches and Flower Drawings by Charles Rennie Mackintosh* (New York: Rizzoli, 1977).

11. James Macaulay, *Hill House: Charles Rennie Mackintosh* (London: Phaidon, 1994), 15.

12. For site plan, see Wendy Kaplan, ed., *Charles Rennie Mackintosh* (New York: Abbeville Press/Glasgow Museums, 1996), 179.

13. J. J. Joass, "On Gardening: With Descriptions of Some Formal Gardens in Scotland," *The Studio* 11 (August 1897), 167–68.

14. Robert Lorimer, cited in Sir Herbert Maxwell, *Scottish Gardens* (London: Edward Arnold, 1908), 188.

15. Margaret Richardson, *The Craft Architects* (New York: Rizzoli, 1983), 45.

16. See Jekyll and Weaver, *Gardens for Small Country Houses*, 89–91, for a critique of Home Place.

17. Edward S. Prior, "Garden-Making," *The Studio* 21 (October 1900), 28, 31.

18. Edward S. Prior, "Garden-Making III: The Conditions of Material," *The Studio* 21 (December 1900), 176.

19. Edward S. Prior, "Garden-Making II: The Conditions of Practice," *The Studio* 21 (November 1900), 95.

20. A partial list of Mallows's commissions includes Joyce Grove, Nettlebed, Oxon (1911); Dalham Hall, Suffolk; Canons Park, Edgware, Middlesex; Crocombe, Happisburgh, Norfolk (1909); and Brackenston, Pembury, Kent (1904), in addition to Tirley Garth, Taporley, Cheshire (1912), and Craig-y-Parc, Pentyrch, Wales (1913).

21. Jekyll and Weaver, *Gardens for Small Country Houses*, xvii.

22. For the life and work of Griggs, see Jerrold Northrop Moore, *F. L. Griggs: The Architecture of Dreams* (Oxford: Clarendon Press, 1999).

23. Griggs illustrated E. V. Boyle's *Seven Gardens and a Palace* (1900), Harry Roberts's *The Chronicle of a Cornish Garden* (1901), and Mary Pamela Milne-Home's *Stray Leaves from a Border Garden* (1901) as well as over a dozen volumes of Macmillan's popular *Highways and Byways* series.

24. C. E. Mallows, "Architectural Gardening," *The Studio* 44 (August 1908), 181–82.

25. C. E. Mallows, "Architectural Gardening IV," *The Studio* 46 (March 1909), 120–21.

26. Clive Aslet, "Tirley Garth," *Country Life* 171 (18 March 1982), 702.

CHAPTER 5. INDIVIDUALITY AND IMAGINATION

1. *Studio Year Book of Decorative Art 1909* (London: The Studio, 1909), 28; C.F.A. Voysey, *Individuality* (London: Chapman and Hall, 1915).

2. John Betjeman, "Charles Francis Annesley Voysey, the Architect of Individualism," *The Architectural Review*, October 1931, 93.

3. For more on Voysey's life and career, consult Wendy Hitchmough, *C.F.A. Voysey* (New York: Phaidon, 1995). There is a large archive of Voysey's architectural work in the Drawings Collection, Royal Institute of British Architects, London, and an archive of his textiles and wallpapers at the Victoria and Albert Museum, London.

4. M. H. Baillie Scott, "On the Characteristics of Mr. C.F.A. Voysey's Architecture," *The Studio* 42 (October 1907), 19.

5. Sir Edwin Lutyens, "Foreword," *The Achitectural Review*, October 1931, 91.

6. T. Raffles Davison, *Modern Homes* (London: George Bell, 1909), 119.

7. Betjeman coined the term Metro-land for the bedroom communities ringing London where Voysey built many of his houses.

8. "An Interview with Mr. C.F.A. Voysey, *The Studio* 1 (September 1893), 232.

9. Jekyll and Weaver, *Gardens for Small Country Houses*, 162, fig. 220.

10. Examples of his garden architecture can be seen at Greyfriars, Lowicks, Norney Grange, Littleholme, Priors Garth, and New Place. There is a discussion of Littleholme in Jekyll and Weaver, *Gardens for Small Country Houses*, 76–80.

11. W. Duggan, "The Gardens at New Place, Haslemere," *The Garden* 85 (6 August 1921), 388.

12. "Some Recent Work of C.F.A. Voysey, an English Architect," *House and Garden* 3 (May 1903), 256.

13. See Muthesius, *Das Englische Haus*, vol. 2, 113, 114, for photographs of these garden houses. Voysey designed summerhouses for Lowicks, which also sports a similar weathercock, and Norney Grange.

14. See planting plan in Jane Brown, "The Garden of New Place," *The Garden* 108 (June 1983), 232, based on file in Gertrude Jekyll Collection, Environmental Design Archives, University of California, Berkeley.

15. See Alan Powers, "Blackwell, Cumbria," *Country Life* 195 (12 July 2001), 86–91.

16. John Betjeman, "Mackay Hugh Baillie Scott," *Journal of the Manx Museum*, 1968, cited in Diane Haigh, *Baillie Scott, The Artistic House* (London: Academy Editions, 1995), 116.

17. "An Ideal Suburban House," *The Studio* 4 (January 1895), 127–32; "The Decoration of the Suburban House," *The Studio* 5 (April 1895), 15–21.

18. M. H. Baillie Scott, *Houses and Gardens* (London: George Newnes, 1906), 1.

19. M. H. Baillie Scott and A. Edgar Beresford, *Houses and Gardens* (London: Architecture Illustrated, 1933), 32.

20. *Houses and Gardens* (1906), 81, 84.

21. *Houses and Gardens* (1906), 82.

22. *Houses and Gardens* (1906), 3, 85.

23. Greenways, Sunningdale (1907); Runton Old Hall, Norfolk (1908); Garden Corner, Guildford (1915).

24. Letter, Baillie Scott to Gertrude Jekyll, 12 August 1907, Gertrude Jekyll Collection, Environmental Design Archives, University of California, Berkeley.

25. "Recent Designs in Domestic Architecture," *The Studio* 51 (December 1910), 222.

26. Tankard and Wood, *Gertrude Jekyll at Munstead Wood*, 136.

27. "The Studio Prize Competitions," *The Studio* 41 (June 1907), 86.

28. Gervase Jackson-Stops, *An English Arcadia 1600–1990* (Washington, D.C.: AIA Press/The National Trust, 1990), 147; A. E. Richardson, in "Snowshill Manor, Gloucestershire," *Country Life* 62 (1 October 1927), 470–77, attributes the design of the garden to Wade.

29. Haigh, *Baillie Scott, The Artistic House*, 69.

CHAPTER 6. THE ART AND CRAFT OF GARDEN-MAKING

1. In *The Art and Craft of Garden-Making*, Mawson designated himself "garden architect"; his autobiography is entitled *The Life and Work of an English Landscape Gardener* in Britain, while the American edition is entitled *The Life and Work of an English Landscape Architect*.

2. Ken Lemmon, "Landscaper of the World: Thomas H. Mawson, a Self-Help Victorian," *Country Life* 175 (10 May 1984), 1318.

3. Thomas H. Mawson, *The Life and Work of an English Landscape Architect* (New York: Charles Scribner's Sons, 1927), 41–42.

4. Geoffrey Beard, *Thomas H. Mawson: A Northern Landscape Architect* (University of Lancaster, 1978), 11.

5. Thornton Manor, Cheshire (1905); Rivington Pike, Bolton (1906), Roynton Cottage, Bolton (1906); The Hill, Hampstead, London (1906).

6. "Since the appearance of *The Formal Garden* by Reginald Blomfield, we have seen no work on the fascinating subject of artistic gardens to be compared in interest with the one under review" (*The Studio* 20 [July 1900], 135.)

7. Mawson, *Life and Work*, 164.

8. Thomas H. Mawson, *The Art and Craft of Garden-Making*, 2nd ed. (London: B. T. Batsford, 1901), xi. Unless otherwise noted, all citations are taken from this edition.

9. Mawson worked with Voysey at Moor Crag, Ghyll Head, Windermere (1898) and Baillie Scott at Blackwell (1902), also in Windermere.

10. Mawson, *The Art and Craft of Garden-Making*, 222.

11. Mawson, *The Art and Craft of Garden-Making*, 224.

12. Dyffryn Gardens, with its magnificent collection of specimen trees, is currently undergoing a full-scale restoration. The layout of the grounds is basically unaltered.

13. Reginald Cory (1871–1934), a longtime benefactor to the Royal Horticultural Society where he bequeathed his extensive horticultural library, was renowned for his work in hybridizing plants. His collection of dahlias, for example, numbered six hundred varieties. Cory was also interested in town planning and had Mawson design a projected model village, Glyn Cory, near Dyffryn.

14. Thomas H. Mawson and E. Prentice Mawson, *The Art and Craft of Garden-Making*, 5th ed. (London: B. T. Batsford, 1926), 386–89.

15. Within three months of the book's initial publication in October 1912, a second, revised edition was printed, with an expanded introduction that included measured drawings that were not completed in time for the first edition. All citations are taken from this edition.

16. Jekyll and Weaver, *Gardens for Small Country Houses*, xxxiii.

17. Jekyll and Weaver, *Gardens for Small Country Houses*, 55–59.

18. Mawson, *The Art and Craft of Garden-Making*, 69.

19. Jekyll and Weaver, *Gardens for Small Country Houses*, 99.

20. Mawson, *The Art and Craft of Garden-Making*, 118–19.

21. Jekyll and Weaver, *Gardens for Small Country Houses*, 147, 158.

22. Mawson, *The Art and Craft of Garden-Making*, 77.

23. Mawson, *The Art and Craft of Garden-Making*, 77.

24. Jekyll and Weaver, *Gardens for Small Country Houses*, 238.

CHAPTER 7. AT HOME WITH TWO MASTER GARDENERS

1. Among Robinson's books, the most important are *The Parks, Promenades, and Gardens of Paris* (1869), *Alpine Flowers for English Gardens* (1870), *The Wild Garden* (1870), *The Subtropical Garden* (1871), *The English Flower Garden* (1883), *Garden Design and Architects' Gardens* (1892), *The Garden Beautiful* (1907), *Gravetye Manor* (1911), *The Virgin's Bower* (1912), and *Home Landscapes* (1914), all published in London by John Murray.

2. For the history of some of Robinson's books, see Judith B. Tankard, "A Perennial Favourite: 'The English Flower Garden'," *Hortus* 17 (Spring 1991), 74–85, and "William Robinson and the Art of the Book," *Hortus* 27 (Autumn 1993), 21–30.

3. Tankard, "A Perennial Favourite," 74–85.

4. Like Robinson, Wilhelm Miller (1869–1938) founded or wrote for several magazines, including *Country Life in America*. His book, *What England Can Teach Us about Gardening* (Garden City: Doubleday, Page, 1911), reflects his travels in England in 1908.

5. *The Studio* 32 (15 July 1904), 174.

6. Robinson's original "Tree and Garden Books," containing plant lists and other information omitted from *Gravetye Manor*, are held in the Lindley Library, London.

7. Robinson thought that Devey's remodeling of Gravetye Manor, undertaken between August 1885 and September 1886 and one of his last commissions, was carelessly done. See Jill Allibone, *George Devey Architect, 1820–1886* (Cambridge: Lutterworth Press, 1991).

8. Letter, Edwin Lutyens to Emily Lutyens, 24 August 1903, cited in Clayre Percy and Jane Ridley, eds., *The Letters of Edwin Lutyens to His Wife Lady Emily* (London: Collins, 1985), 106.

9. William Robinson, "In the Garden," *Country Life* 34 (4 October 1913), 452.

10. Robinson, *Gravetye Manor*, 96.

11. William Robinson, "The Flower Garden at Gravetye Manor," *Country Life* 32 (28 September 1912), 409.

12. Henry James, *Pictures and Text* (New York: Harper and Brothers, 1893), 88–89.

13. Robinson, "The Flower Garden at Gravetye Manor," 411.

14. Robinson, *Gravetye Manor*, 95.

15. Judith B. Tankard, "Moonscape," *Country Life* 190 (9 May 1996), 72–73.

16. Last Will and Testament of William Robinson, 17 January 1928, 7, H. M. Probate Registry, London.

17. Peter Herbert, "Foreword," *The Wild Garden*, new ed. (New York: Sagapress, 1994), and in conversation with the author.

18. Peter Savage, *Lorimer and the Edinburgh Craft Designers* (Edinburgh: Paul Harris, 1980), 25.

19. See Judith B. Tankard, "The Garden Before Munstead Wood," *Hortus* 20 (Winter 1991), 17–26, for a detailed description.

20. William Goldring, "Munstead, Godalming," *The Garden* 22 (26 August 1882), 191–92.

21. Jekyll and Weaver, *Gardens for Small Country Houses*, 36.

22. Gertrude Jekyll, *Colour in the Flower Garden* (London: Country Life, 1908), 55.

23. See Judith B. Tankard, "Miss Jekyll's True Colours," *Country Life* 191 (15 May 1997), 140–43 for period views of these gardens in color.

24. Herbert Baker, *Architecture and Personalities* (London: Country Life, 1944), 16.

25. Gertrude Jekyll, *Home and Garden* (London: Longmans, Green, 1900), 1.

26. Despite the simplicity of her house, it cost Gertrude Jekyll almost £4,000, a considerable sum in 1897.

CHAPTER 8. A PERFECT HOUSE AND GARDEN

1. Judith B. Tankard, "Gardening with *Country Life*," *Hortus* 30 (Summer 1994), 72–86.
2. See Fenja Gunn, "Jekyll's Country Life Style," *Country Life* 187 (26 August 1993), 46–49, for a discussion of Lutyens's commissions for Edward Hudson.
3. Christopher Hussey, *The Life of Sir Edwin Lutyens* (London: Country Life; New York: Charles Scribner's, 1950), 95.
4. Hussey, *Life of Lutyens*, 96.
5. [H. Avray Tipping?], "A House and a Garden," *Country Life* 13 (9 May 1903), 602–11. In his discussion of Deanery Garden, T. Raffles Davidson, in *Modern Homes* (London: George Bell, 1909), gives credit to Jekyll's role: "It is a signal tribute to the ability of its architect, Mr. E. L. Lutyens, to create a house, and to Miss Gertrude Jekyll to create a garden which are so entirely in sympathy with each other."
6. Lawrence Weaver, *Houses of E. L. Lutyens* (London: Country Life, 1913), 58.
7. Jekyll and Weaver, *Gardens for Small Country Houses*, 26.
8. After being in continuous private ownership, Goddards became the headquarters of the Lutyens Trust in 1991, and is now under the management of the Landmark Trust.
9. Weaver, *Houses of E. L. Lutyens*, 39.
10. Lawrence Weaver, "Marshcourt, Hampshire," *Country Life* 33 (19 April 1913), 562.
11. Jekyll and Weaver, *Gardens for Small Country Houses*, 158.
12. H. Avray Tipping, "Millmead, Bramley," *Country Life* 21 (11 May 1907), 677.
13. Jekyll and Weaver, *Gardens for Small Country Houses*, 1–2. The property had had an unglamorous history, with pigs being kept there at one time. The Jacobean cottages were demolished in 1898.
14. Tipping, "Millmead, Bramley," 676.
15. Jekyll and Weaver, *Gardens for Small Country Houses*, 2–3.
16. Jekyll and Weaver, *Gardens for Small Country Houses*, 2–3.
17. Unlike many of the earlier Lutyens and Jekyll projects, there are ample working drawings and notes pertaining to the gardens at Folly Farm in the Gertrude Jekyll Collection, Environmental Design Archives, University of California, Berkeley. Curiously, most of the plans relate to the 1906 scheme and little information exists for the later, more important, scheme of 1912. Handwritten notes on the drawings, such as "Steps up to the Croquet Court?," confirm Jekyll's involvement in design decisions as well as the planting.
18. The one at Westbury Court, Gloucestershire, is one of the few remaining examples of this type of water feature. Most were destroyed by "Capability" Brown in the eighteenth century, when the landscape style replaced formality in garden design.

19. Christopher Hussey, "Folly Farm," *Country Life* 51 (28 January 1922), 114.
20. In the 1970s, the American landscape architect Lanning Roper simplified the plantings, replacing high-maintenance flowers with perennials, giving Folly Farm an updated look. See Lanning Roper, "A Garden of Vistas," *Country Life* 157 (15 May 1975), 1230–32.

CHAPTER 9. BEYOND THE BORDERS

1. Lawrence Weaver, "Ardkinglas," *Country Life* 29 (27 May 1911), 746.
2. The September 27, 1912, issue of *Country Life* contains a special supplement devoted to the work of Robert Lorimer.
3. Whinfold, Hascombe, Surrey (1898); High Barn, Hascombe, Surrey (1901); Brackenburgh, Penrith, Cumberland (1901); and Barton Hartshorn, Buckingham, Oxfordshire (1902).
4. Jekyll and Weaver, *Gardens for Small Country Houses*, xliii; see also, Lawrence Weaver, "The Walled Garden at Edzell Castle," *Country Life* 32 (14 December 1914), 859–62.
5. Christopher Hussey, *The Work of Sir Robert Lorimer* (London: Country Life, 1931), 7, 17, 18.
6. Robert Lorimer, "On Scottish Gardens," *The Architectural Review*, November 1899, 194–205, as cited in Peter Savage, "Lorimer and the Garden Heritage of Scotland," *Garden History, Journal of the Garden History Society* 5 (Summer 1977), 30.
7. Hussey, *The Work of Robert Lorimer*, 24.
8. Hew Lorimer, *Kellie Castle and Garden* (National Trust for Scotland, 1985), 4.
9. Hussey, *The Work of Robert Lorimer*, 15.
10. Elgood and Jekyll, *Some English Gardens*, 48, 50.
11. Kathleen Sayer, "Kellie Castle Garden in Spring," *Hortus* 29 (Spring 1994), 46–52.
12. "Earlshall, Fifeshire, the Seat of Mr. R. W. Mackenzie," *Country Life* 17 (1 July 1905), 942–50.
13. Hussey, *The Work of Robert Lorimer*, 24; Peter Verney, *The Gardens of Scotland* (London: B. T. Batsford, 1976), 77.
14. Peter Savage, *Lorimer and the Edinburgh Craft Designers* (Edinburgh: Paul Harris, 1980), 11.
15. All four properties are owned by The National Trust.
16. Christopher Hussey, "Gardener and Antiquary," *Country Life* 74 (25 November 1933), 567.
17. Lady Congreve, "The Late H. Avray Tipping, a Personal Recollection," *Country Life* 74 (25 November 1933), 566–67.
18. [H. A. Tipping], "Mathern Palace, Monmouthshire," *Country Life* 28 (19 November 1910), 725.
19. H. Avray Tipping, *English Gardens* (London: Country Life, 1925), 219.
20. H. Avray Tipping, *The Garden of To-Day* (London: Martin

Hopkinson, 1933), 44.

21. See Tipping, *English Gardens*, 225–38, for garden plan and photographs of Mounton House.

22. H. Avray Tipping, "High Glanau, Monmouthshire" *Country Life* 65 (8 June 1929), 829.

23. H. Avray Tipping, "High Glanau II, Monmouthshire," *Country Life* 65 (15 June 1929), 856.

24. David Wheeler, "A Corner of Wales That Is Forever England," *Country Life* 192 (16 July 1998), 61.

25. C. H. Reilly, *Representative British Architects of the Present Day* (London: Batsford, 1931), 93.

26. In 1919 he published a book on *Cottage Building in Cob, Pisé, Chalk and Clay*.

27. Richard Haslam, *Clough Williams-Ellis: RIBA Drawings Collection Monographs* (London: Academy, 1996) for examples of his work.

28. *England and the Octopus* (London: Geoffrey Bles, 1928). He also wrote (with his wife, Amabel Williams-Ellis) *The Pleasures of Architecture* (London: Jonathan Cape, 1924), and his autobiography *Architect Errant* (London: Constable, 1971).

29. Jekyll and Hussey, *Garden Ornament*, 365.

30. Christopher Hussey, "Plas Brondanw, Merionethshire," *Country Life* 69 (31 January 1931), 136.

31. Gertrude Knoblock, whose studio was located in London, designed fountain figures with cherubs and small children that were popular in American gardens as well as British ones in the 1930s.

CHAPTER 10. COLOR IN THE FLOWER GARDEN

1. The famous painting, featuring two young girls at twilight holding lighted paper lanterns among the lilies and carnations, is at the Tate Gallery, London.

2. Henry James, "Our Artists in Europe," *Harper's New Monthly Magazine* 79 (June 1889), 58.

3. Parsons's home, now called Luggers Hall, has fully restored gardens and offers bed and breakfast accommodations.

4. Even though Parsons's career as a garden designer is elusive, he is known to have designed gardens for Percy's Wyndham at Philip Webb's Clouds, Wiltshire (now demolished); Great Chatfield Manor, Wiltshire; Hartpury House, Gloucestershire (with Thomas Mawson), and others. See Diana Baskervyle-Glegg, "Bulbs Shine Bright in Broadway," *Country Life* 192 (29 January 1998), 40–43, and Nicole Milette, *Parsons, Partridge, Tudway: An Unsuspected Garden Design Partnership, 1884–1914* (York: Institute of Advanced Architectural Studies, 1995).

5. Giles Edgerton, "Mary Anderson 'At Home' in the Cotswolds," *Arts & Decoration*, March 1937, 12–15.

6. See Bryan N. Brooke, "Willmott, Parsons, and *Genus Rosa, The Garden* 112 (October 1987), 455–58. Parsons's original watercolors were presented to the Royal Horticultural Society's Lindley Library through the Reginald Cory Bequest.

7. She shared her bounty with her younger sister, Rose, who married Robert Berkeley of Berkeley Castle, Glos., and was also an accomplished gardener. For biographical details, see Audrey Le Lièvre's *Miss Willmott of Warley Place* (London: Faber and Faber, 1980).

8. Norah Lindsay, "The Manor House, Sutton Courtenay, Berks.," *Country Life* 69 (16 May 1931), 610.

9. Nellie B. Allen, an American garden designer, noted these colors on the back of her framed photograph of Lindsay's Long Garden.

10. T. [H. Avray Tipping], "Hestercombe, Somerset," *Country Life* 24 (17 October 1908), 528. Tipping attributes the garden entirely to Lutyens, without mentioning Jekyll. Christopher Hussey's articles in *Country Life* twenty years later, however, sing her praises.

11. To read about the recent restoration, see Rosamund Wallinger, *Gertrude Jekyll's Lost Garden: The Restoration of an Edwardian Masterpiece* (Woodbridge, Suffolk: Garden Art Press, 2000).

12. Graham Stuart Thomas, "Foreword," Tankard and Wood, *Gertrude Jekyll at Munstead Wood*, xi–xii.

13. Penelope Hobhouse, ed., *Gertrude Jekyll on Gardening* (Boston: David R. Godine, 1984), 281.

14. Helen Dillon, *Garden Artistry* (New York: Macmillan, 1995), 9.

15. Jekyll, *Colour in the Flower Garden*, v1.

16. Dillon, *Garden Artistry*, 13.

17. Jekyll, *Colour in the Flower Garden*, 90.

18. Dillon, *Garden Artistry*, 65.

CHAPTER 11. CRAFTSMAN STYLE

1. See Jens Jensen, *Siftings* (1939), reprinted by Johns Hopkins Press, 1990, and O. C. Simonds, *Landscape Gardening* (1920), reprinted by University of Massachusetts Press, 2000.

2. Mabel Tuke Priestman, "History of the Arts and Crafts Movement in America," *House Beautiful*, October and November 1906, as reprinted in *History of the Arts and Crafts Movement in America* (Berkeley: The Arts and Crafts Press, 1996), 21.

3. Mark Alan Hewitt, *Gustav Stickley's Craftsman Farms: The Quest for an Arts and Crafts Utopia* (Syracuse: Syracuse University Press, 2001), 1.

4. Natalie Curtis, "The New Log House at Craftsman Farms: An Architectural Development of the Log Cabin," *The Craftsman* 21 (November 1911), 201.

5. "Craftsman Farms: Its Development and Future," *The Craftsman* 25 (October 1913), 8–15.

6. "The Growing Individuality of the American Garden," *The Craftsman* 20 (April 1911), 54–62.

7. As Baillie Scott explained in *Houses and Gardens* (1933), "The house in America is one of those for which we merely supplied the drawings." It was built by an architect associated with the firm of McKim, Mead and White.

8. See David Cathers, "The Close: Old England in New Jersey," *American Bungalow* 29 (Spring 2001), 9–14.

9. Alan Crawford, *C. R. Ashbee: Architect, Designer and Romantic Socialist* (New Haven: Yale University Press, 1985), 407.

10. Frank Lloyd Wright, "Concerning Landscape Architecture," *Frank Lloyd Wright Collected Writings, 1894–1930*. Courtesy of John Arthur, who provided this reference.

11. Virginia A. Green, *The Architecture of Howard Van Doren Shaw* (Chicago: Chicago Review Press, 1998), 13.

12. See Suzanne Turner, *The Landscape of Ragdale, Home of the Howard Van Doren Shaw Family and the Ragdale Foundation* (Cultural Landscape Report, privately printed, 2002) and Alice Hayes and Susan Moon, *Ragdale, A History and Guide* (Berkeley: Open Books/Ragdale Foundation, 1990).

13. Ragdale has always been the home of artists, first with members of Shaw's family, and now it is an artists' retreat. One of his daughters, Sylvia Shaw Judson, was a renowned sculptor, whose sculptural pieces enhance the site today.

14. Charles Keeler, *The Simple Home* (1904; reprint by Peregrine Smith, 1979), 15.

15. They may have visited the Japanese pavilion at the World's Columbian Exposition in Chicago in 1893. See Edward R. Bosley, "Greene and Greene: The British Connection," *The Tabby: A Chronicle of the Arts and Crafts Movement* 3 (July–August 1997), 7.

16. Bosley, "Greene and Greene," 16–17.

17. David C. Streatfield, "Echoes of England and Italy 'On the Edge of the World': Green Gables and Charles Greene," *Journal of Garden History* 2 (October–December 1982), 380.

18. Thaisa Way, *Arts and Crafts Gardens in California* (Charlottesville: University of Virginia M. A. Thesis, 1991), 1.

19. David C. Streatfield, *California Gardens: Creating a New Eden* (New York: Abbeville Press, 1994), 83.

CHAPTER 12. BEAUTIFUL GARDENS IN AMERICA

1. Louise Shelton, *Beautiful Gardens in America* (New York: Charles Scribner's Sons, 1915), 7.

2. For a comprehensive history, see May Brawley Hill, *Grandmother's Garden: The Old-Fashioned American Garden, 1865–1915* (New York: Abrams, 1995).

3. See Virginia Lopez Begg, "Mabel Osgood Wright: The Friendship of Nature and the Commuter's Wife," *Journal of the New England Garden History Society* 5 (1997), 35–41, for the role of women in garden literature.

4. Mariana Griswold Van Rensselaer, *Art Out-of-Doors* (New York: Charles Scribner's, 1893), 8.

5. See Judith B. Tankard, "Defining Their Turf: Pioneer Women Landscape Designers," *Bard Studies in Decorative Arts* 8 (Fall–Winter 2000–2001), 31–53.

6. Frances Duncan, "The Gardens of Cornish," *The Century Magazine*, May 1906, 3–19.

7. See Alma Gilbert and Judith Tankard, *A Place of Beauty: The Artists and Gardens of the Cornish Colony* (Berkeley: Ten Speed Press, 2000), 69–75.

8. See Judith B. Tankard, "Henry Davis Sleeper's Gardens at Beauport," *Journal of the New England Garden History Society* 10 (2002), 30–43.

9. Judith B. Tankard, "Nellie B. Allen," *Pioneers of American Landscape Design* (New York: McGraw-Hill, 2000).

10. Rose Standish Nichols, *English Pleasure Gardens* (Boston: David R. Godine, 2003), 255.

11. Nichols designed approximately seventy gardens, but little is known about most of them because her office records were discarded after her death.

12. Louise Beebe Wilder, *Adventures in a Suburban Garden* (Garden City: Doubleday, 1931), 53.

13. The other commissions were for a woodland garden in Greenwich, Conn., and an elaborate terraced garden (unbuilt) near Cincinnati, Ohio.

14. In the 1920s, Jekyll received the Old Glebe House commission from Standard Oil heiress Annie Burr Jennings, in much the same spirit as Americans today mistakenly look to English designers for their inspiration.

15. Notebooks, 1909–1912, Henry Francis du Pont Winterthur Museum Archives, Delaware. See also Denise Magnani, *The Winterthur Garden* (New York: Harry N. Abrams, 1995).

16. Judith B. Tankard, "Shelburne Farms, the Family Gardens," *Old-House Interiors*, Fall 1998, 66–73.

17. See Balmori, McGuire, and McPeck, *Beatrix Farrand's American Landscapes* (New York: Sagapress, 1985) for an overview of her career.

18. Lamar Sparks, "A Landscape Architect Discusses Gardens," *Better Homes and Gardens*, November 1930, 20.

19. Ellen Shipman, "Garden Notebook," unpublished manuscript, author's collection, 38.

Selected Bibliography

Allan, Mea. *William Robinson, 1838–1935: Father of the English Flower Garden*. London: Faber and Faber, 1982

Anscombe, Isabelle. *Arts and Crafts Style*. New York: Rizzoli, 1991

___, and Charlotte Gere. *Arts and Crafts in Britain and America*. New York: Rizzoli, 1978

Aslet, Clive. *The Last Country Houses*. New Haven: Yale University Press, 1982

Ayers, Dianne, Timothey Hansen, et al. *American Arts and Crafts Textiles*. New York: Harry N. Abrams, 2002

Baker, Derek. *The Flowers of William Morris*. London: Barn Elms, 1996

Balmori, Diana, Diane K. McGuire, and Eleanor M. McPeck. *Beatrix Farrand's American Landscapes: Her Gardens and Campuses*. New York: Sagapress, 1985

Birnbaum, Charles A., ed. *Pioneers of American Landscape Design*. New York: McGraw-Hill, 2000

Bisgrove, Richard. *The Gardens of Gertrude Jekyll*. Boston: Little, Brown, 1992

Blomfield, Reginald. *The Formal Garden in England*. London: Macmillan, 1892

Bosley, Edward R. *Gamble House: Greene and Greene*. London: Phaidon, 1992

___. *Greene and Greene*. London:: Phaidon, 2000

Bowman, Leslie Greene. *American Arts and Crafts: Virtue in Design*. Boston: Bulfinch Press/Los Angeles County Museum, 1990

Brandon-Jones, John, et al. *C.F.A. Voysey: Architect and Designer, 1857–1941*. London: Lund Humphries, 1978

Brown, Jane. *The Art and Architecture of English Gardens*. New York: Rizzoli, 1989

___. *The English Garden through the Twentieth Century*. Woodbridge, Suffolk: Garden Art Press, 1999

___. *Gardens of a Golden Afternoon: The Partnership of Gertrude Jekyll and Edwin Lutyens*. New York: Penguin, 1995

Butler, A.S.G. *The Lutyens Memorial: The Architecture of Sir Edwin Lutyens*, 3 vols. London: Country Life, 1950

Callen, Anthea. *Women Artists of the Arts and Crafts Movement*. New York: Pantheon, 1979

Clark, Robert Judson, ed. *The Arts and Crafts Movement in America, 1876–1916*. Princeton: Princeton University Press, 1972

Comino, Mary. *Gimson and the Barnsleys: 'Wonderful Furniture of a Commonplace Kind.'* New York: Van Nostrand Reinhold, 1982

Cornforth, John. *The Inspiration of the Past: Country House Taste in the Twentieth Century*. New York: Viking Penguin, 1985

Cummings, Elizabeth, and Wendy Kaplan. *The Arts and Crafts Movement*. New York: Thames and Hudson, 1991

Darke, Rick. *In Harmony with Nature: Lessons from the Arts and Crafts Garden*. New York: Friedman/Fairfax, 2000

Dash, Robert. *Notes from Madoo: Making a Garden in the Hamptons*. Boston: Houghton Mifflin, 2000

Davey, Peter. *Arts and Crafts Architecture*. New York: Phaidon, 1995

Davison, T. Raffles. *Modern Homes: Selected Examples of Dwelling Houses*. London: George Bell, 1909

Dillon, Helen. *Garden Artistry: Secrets of Designing and Planting a Small Garden*. New York: Macmillan, 1995

Dobyns, Winifred Starr. *California Gardens*. New York: Macmillan, 1931

Drury, Michael. *Wandering Architects: In Pursuit of an Arts and Crafts Ideal*. Stamford, Lincs.: Shaun Tyas, 2000

Earle, Alice Morse. *Old-Time Gardens Newly Set Forth*. New York: Macmillan, 1901

Edward, Brian. *Goddards: Sir Edwin Lutyens*. London: Phaidon, 1996

Edwards, Paul, and Katherine Swift. *Pergolas, Arbours, and Arches: Their History and How To Make Them*. London: Barn Elms, 2001

Elgood, George S., and Gertrude Jekyll. *Some English Gardens*. London: Longmans, Green, 1904

Elliott, Brent. *The Country House Garden from the Archives of Country Life, 1897–1939*. London: Mitchell Beazley, 1995

___. *Victorian Gardens*. London: Batsford, 1986

Gere, Charlotte, and Lesley Hoskins. *The House Beautiful: Oscar Wilde and the Aesthetic Interior*. London: Lund Humphries/Geffrye Museum, 2000

Gilbert, Alma M., and Judith B. Tankard. *A Place of Beauty: The Artists and Gardens of the Cornish Colony*. Berkeley: Ten Speed Press, 2000

Girouard, Mark. *Sweetness and Light: The Queen Anne Movement, 1860–1900*. New Haven: Yale University Press, 1984

Godfrey, Walter H. *Gardens in the Making*. London: Batsford, 1914

Gow, Ian. *Scottish Houses and Gardens from the Archives of Country Life*. London: Aurum Press, 1997

Gradidge, Roderick. *Dream Houses: The Edwardian Ideal*. London: Constable, 1980

Greene, Virginia A. *The Architecture of Howard Van Doren Shaw*. Chicago: Chicago Review Press, 1998

Greensted, Mary. *The Arts and Crafts Movement in the Cotswolds*. Stroud: Alan Sutton, 1993

Griggs, F. L., W. R. Lethaby, and Alfred H. Powell. *Ernest Gimson, His Life and Work*. Stratford-upon-Avon: Shakespeare Head Press, 1924

Griswold, Mac, and Eleanor Weller. *The Golden Age of American Gardens*. New York: Harry N. Abrams, 1992

Gunn, Fenja. *The Lost Gardens of Gertrude Jekyll*. New York: Macmillan, 1991

Haigh, Diane. *Baillie Scott: The Artistic House*. London: Academy, 1995

Hamilton, Jill, Penny Hart, and John Simmons. *The Gardens of William Morris*. New York: Stewart, Tabori and Chang, 1998

Haslam, Richard. *Clough Williams-Ellis*. London: Academy, 1996

Head, Heart and Hand: Elbert Hubbard and the Roycrofters. Rochester: University of Rochester Press, 1994

Hewitt, Mark Alan. *The Architect and the American Country House*. New Haven: Yale University Press, 1990

___. *Gustav Stickley's Craftsman Farms: The Quest for an Arts and*

Crafts Utopia. Syracuse: Syracuse University Press, 2001

Hill, May Brawley. *Furnishing the Old-Fashioned Garden: Three Centuries of American Summerhouses, Dovecotes, Pergolas, Privies, Fences, and Birdhouses*. New York: Harry N. Abrams, 1998

___. *Grandmother's Garden: The Old-Fashioned American Garden, 1865–1915*. New York: Harry N. Abrams, 1995

Hitchmough, Wendy. *Arts and Crafts Gardens*. New York: Rizzoli, 1997

___. *The Arts and Crafts Lifestyle and Design*. New York: Watson-Guptill, 2000

___. *C.F.A. Voysey*. New York: Phaidon, 1995

Hobhouse, Penelope. *Colour in Your Garden* (1985). London: Frances Lincoln, 2003

___. *Natural Planting*. New York: Henry Holt, 1997

___, and Christopher Wood. *Painted Gardens: English Watercolours, 1850–1914*. London: Michael Joseph, 1988

Hollamby, Edward. *Red House: Philip Webb*. New York: Van Nostrand Reinhold, 1991

Holme, Charles, ed. *The Gardens of England in the Midland and Eastern Counties, The Gardens of England in the Northern Counties, The Gardens of England in the Southern and Western Counties*. London: The Studio, 1907–11

Hussey, Christopher. *The Work of Sir Robert Lorimer*. London: Country Life, 1931

Israel, Barbara. *Antique Garden Ornament: Two Centuries of American Taste*. New York: Harry N. Abrams, 1999

Jekyll, Gertrude. *Colour in the Flower Garden*. London: Country Life, 1908

___. *Home and Garden*. London: Longmans, Green, 1900

___, and Christopher Hussey. *Garden Ornament*. London: Country Life, 1927

___, and Lawrence Weaver. *Gardens for Small Country Houses*. London: Country Life, 1912

Jewson, Norman. *By Chance I Did Rove* (1951). Warwick: privately printed, 1973

Kaplan, Wendy. *The Art That Is Life: The Arts and Crafts Movement in America, 1875–1920*. Boston: Museum of Fine Arts, 1987

___, ed. *Charles Rennie Mackintosh*. New York: Abbeville Press/Glasgow Museums, 1996

Lambourne, Lionel. *Utopian Craftsmen: The Arts and Crafts Movement from the Cotswolds to Chicago*. Salt Lake City: Peregrine Smith, 1980

Le Lièvre, Audrey. *Miss Willmott of Warley Place: Her Life and Her Gardens*. London: Faber and Faber, 1980

Lees-Milne, James. *Some Cotswold Country Houses: A Personal Selection*. Stanbridge, Dorset: Dovecote Press, 1987

Lethaby, William R. *Philip Webb and His Work*. Oxford: Oxford University Press, 1935

Leyland, John, and H. Avray Tipping, eds. *Gardens Old and New: The Country House and Its Garden Environment*, 3 vols. London: Country Life, 1901–07

Lloyd, Nathaniel. *Garden Craftsmanship in Yew and Box*. London: Ernest Benn, 1925

Lowell, Guy. *American Gardens*. Boston: Bates, 1902

Macaulay, James. *Hill House: Charles Rennie Mackintosh*. London: Phaidon, 1994

MacCarthy, Fiona. *William Morris: A Life for Our Time*. New York: Alfred A. Knopf, 1995

Mackail, J. W. *The Life of William Morris* (1899). New York: Benjamin Blom, 1968

Mawson, Thomas. *The Art and Craft of Garden-Making*. London: Batsford, 1901

___. *The Life and Work of an English Landscape Gardener*. New York: Scribner's, 1927

Meyer, Marilee Boyd, et al. *Inspiring Reform: Boston's Arts and Crafts Movement*. New York: Harry N. Abrams/Davis Museum, 1997

Miller, Wilhelm. *What England Can Teach Us about Gardening*. Garden City: Doubleday, Page, 1911

Morgan, Keith N. *Shaping an American Landscape: The Art and Architecture of Charles A. Platt*. Hanover: University Press of New England, 1995

Morris, May, ed. *The Collected Works of William Morris*. London: Longmans, Green, 1910–15

Murmann, Eugene O. *California Gardens*. Los Angeles: Murmann, 1914

Musson, Jeremy. *The English Manor House from the Archives of Country Life*. London: Aurum Press, 1999

Muthesius, Hermann. *The English House* (abridged version of *Das Englische Haus*, 3 vols., Berlin: Wasmuth, 1904–05), Janet Seligman, trans. New York: Rizzoli, 1979

Naylor, Gillian. *The Arts and Crafts Movement: A Study of Its Sources, Ideals and Influence on Design History*. London: Studio Vista, 1971

Newton, William Godfrey. *The Work of Ernest Newton*. London: Architectural Press, 1925

Nichols, Rose Standish. *English Pleasure Gardens* (1902). Boston: David R. Godine, 2003

Otis, Denise. *Grounds for Pleasure: Four Centuries of the American Garden*. New York: Harry N. Abrams, 2002

Ottewill, David. *The Edwardian Garden*. New Haven: Yale University Press, 1989

Parry, Linda. *Textiles of the Arts and Crafts Movement*. London: Thames and Hudson, 1988

___, ed. *William Morris*. London: Victoria and Albert Museum, 1996

___. *William Morris and the Arts and Crafts Movement: A Sourcebook*. London: Studio Editions, 1989

Pevsner, Nikolaus. *Pioneers of Modern Design from William Morris to Walter Gropius*. New York: Museum of Modern Art, 1949

Phillips, R. Randal. *Small Country Houses of To-Day*, vol. 3. London: Country Life, 1925

Richardson, Margaret. *The Craft Architects*. New York: Rizzoli, 1983

Robinson, William. *The English Flower Garden*. London: John Murray, 1883

___. *Garden Design and Architects' Gardens*. London: John Murray, 1892

___. *Gravetye Manor, or Twenty Years' Work around an Old Manor*

House (1911). New York: Sagapress, 1984

___. *The Wild Garden* (1870). New York: Sagapress, 1994

Savage, Peter. *Lorimer and the Edinburgh Crafts Designers.* Edinburgh: Paul Harris, 1980

Saville, Diana. *Gardens for Small Country Houses.* New York: Viking, 1988

Scott, M. H. Baillie. *Houses and Gardens.* London: George Newnes, 1906

___ and E. Edgar Beresford. *Houses and Gardens.* London: Architecture Illustrated, 1933

Scott-James, Anne. *The Cottage Garden.* London: Penguin Books, 1982

Sedding, John. *Garden-Craft Old and New* (1890). London: John Lane, 1901

Shelton, Louise. *Beautiful Gardens in America.* New York: Scribners, 1915, 1924

Smith, Bruce and Alexander Vertikoff. *Greene and Greene Masterworks.* San Francisco: Chronicle Books, 1998

Sparrow, Walter Shaw, ed. *The British Home of To-Day: A Book of Modern Domestic Architecture and the Applied Arts.* New York: Armstrong, 1904

___. *The Modern Home: A Book of British Domestic Architecture for Moderate Incomes.* London: Hodder and Stoughton, c. 1909

___. *Our Homes and How To Make the Best of Them.* London: Hodder and Stoughton, 1909

Spens, Michael, ed. *High Art and Low Life: The Studio and the Fin de Siècle.* London: Victoria and Albert Museum, 1993

Stamp, Gavin. *Edwin Lutyens: Country Houses.* New York: Monacelli Press, 2001

Stickley, Gustav. *Craftsman Homes.* New York: Craftsman Publishing, 1909

Streatfield, David C. *California Gardens: Creating a New Eden.* New York: Abbeville Press, 1994

Strong, Roy. *Country Life 1897–1997: The English Arcadia.* London: C. L. Bates, 1996

Studio Yearbook of Decorative Art. London: The Studio, 1906–60

Symonds, Johanna. *Catalogue of the Drawings Collection of the Royal Institute of British Architects: C.F.A. Voysey.* London: D. C. Heath, 1978

Tamulevich, Susan. *Dumbarton Oaks: Garden Into Art.* New York: Monacelli Press, 2001

Tankard, Judith B. *The Gardens of Ellen Biddle Shipman.* New York: Harry N. Abrams/Sagapress, 1996

___ , and Martin A. Wood. *Gertrude Jekyll at Munstead Wood.* New York: Sagapress, 1996

___, and Michael R. Van Valkenburgh. *Gertrude Jekyll: A Vision of Garden and Wood.* New York: Harry N. Abrams/Sagapress, 1989

Thorne, Martha, ed. *David Adler, Architect: The Elements of Style.* New Haven: Yale University Press, 2002

Tipping, H. Avray. *English Gardens.* London: Country Life, 1925

___. *The Garden of To-Day.* London: Martin Hopkinson, 1933

Tooley, Michael, and Primrose Arnander, eds. *Gertrude Jekyll: Essays on the Life of a Working Amateur.* Durham: Michaelmas Books, 1996

Trapp, Kenneth R., ed. *The Arts and Crafts Movement in California: Living the Good Life.* New York: Abbeville Press, 1993

Triggs, H. Inigo. *Formal Gardens in England and Scotland.* London: Batsford, 1902

Triggs, Oscar Lovell. *Chapters in the History of the Arts and Crafts Movement* (1902). New York: Benjamin Blom, 1971

Truscott, James. *Private Gardens of Scotland.* New York: Harmony Books, 1988

Vallance, Aymer. *William Morris: His Art, His Writings, and His Public Life.* London: George Bell and Sons, 1897

Voysey, Charles Francis Annesley. *Individuality* (1915). Shaftesbury: Element Books, 1986

Wallinger, Rosamund. *Gertrude Jekyll's Lost Garden: The Restoration of an Edwardian Masterpiece.* Woodbridge, Suffolk: Garden Art Press, 2000

Weaver, Lawrence, ed. *The House and Its Equipment.* London: Country Life, 1911

___.*Houses and Gardens by E. L. Lutyens.* London: Country Life, 1913

___ , ed. *Small Country Houses of To-Day.* London: Country Life, 1910

___.ed. *Small Country Houses of To-Day*, vol. 2. London: Country Life, 1919

___.ed. *Small Country Houses: Their Repair and Enlargement.* London: Country Life, 1914

Whalley, Robin, and Anne Jennings. *Knot Gardens and Parterres.* London: Barn Elms, 1998

Wheeler, David. *Over the Hills from Broadway: Images of Cotswold Gardens.* Stroud: Alan Sutton, 1991

Whittle, Elisabeth. *The Historic Gardens of Wales.* London: HMSO, 1992

Wilder, Louise Beebe. *Colour in My Garden* (1918). Boston: Atlantic Monthy Press, 1990

Wilhide, Elizabeth. *William Morris: Décor and Design.* New York: Harry N. Abrams, 1991

Williams-Ellis, Clough. *Architect Errant.* London: Constable, 1971

Winter, Robert, ed. *Toward a Simpler Way of Life: The Arts and Crafts Architects of California.* Berkeley: University of California Press, 1997

Wood, Christopher. *Paradise Lost: Paintings of English Country Life and Landscape, 1850–1914.* New York: Crescent Books, 1993

Woodbridge, Sally. *Bernard Maybeck: Visionary Architect.* New York: Abbeville Press, 1992

Wright, Frank Lloyd. *An Autobiography.* New York: Longmans, Green, 1932

___.*The Natural House.* New York: Horizon Press, 1954

Houses and Gardens To Visit

For further information, consult Peter King, editor, *The Good Gardens Guide* (Bloomsbury); *Gardens of England and Wales Open for Charity* (National Gardens Scheme, www.ngs.org.uk); The National Trust (www.nationaltrust.org.uk); The National Trust for Scotland (www.nts.org.uk); Scotland's Gardens Scheme (www.gardensofscotland.org)

ATHELHAMPTON HOUSE GARDENS
  Dorchester
  Dorset DT2 7LG
  01305–848363
  www.athelhampton.co.uk

BERKELEY CASTLE
  Gloucestershire
  01453–810332

BLACKWELL (BAILLIE SCOTT)
  Bowness-on-Windermere
  Cumbria LA23 3JR
  01539–446139
  www.blackwell.org

BRICKWALL
  The Frewen Educational Trust
  Northiam
  East Sussex TN31 6NL
  01797–253388

BRYAN'S GROUND
(D. WHEELER AND S. DORRELL)
  Stapleton
  Herefordshire LD8 2LP
  01544–260001
  www.bryansground.co.uk

CLIVEDEN
  Taplow
  Berkshire SL6 0JA
  www.nationaltrust.org.uk

COLETON FISHACRE (O. MILNE)
  Kingswear
  Devon TQ6 0EQ
  01803–752466
  www.nationaltrust.org.uk

COMBEND MANOR
(S. BARNSLEY AND G. JEKYLL)
  Elkstone
  Gloucestershire GL53 9PT

COTSWOLD FARM (N. JEWSON)
  Duntisbourne Abbots
  Gloucestershire GL7 7JS
  01285–821857
  by appointment only

CRAIG-Y-PARC (C. E. MALLOWS)
  Pentyrch
  Glamorgan CF15 9NB
  02920–890397
  by appointment only

CRATHES CASTLE
  Banchory
  Aberdeenshire AB31 5QJ
  01330–844525
  www.nts.org.uk

DILLON GARDEN
  45 Sandford Road
  Ranelagh
  Dublin 6
  www.dillongarden.com

DRAKESTONE HOUSE (O. MILNE)
  Stinchcombe
  Gloucestershire GL11 6AS
  01453–542140

DYFFRYN GARDENS (T. MAWSON)
  St. Nicholas
  Vale of Glamorgan
  Cardiff
  02920–593328
  www.dyffryngardens.org.uk

EARLSHALL (R. LORIMER)
  Leuchars
  Fife
  01334–839205

EDZELL CASTLE
  Brechin
  Angus DD9 7UE
  01356–648631
  www.historic-scotland.gov.uk

FOLLY FARM (LUTYENS AND JEKYLL)
  Sulhamstead
  Berkshire RG7 4DF
  01635–841541

GODDARDS (LUTYENS AND JEKYLL)
  The Landmark Trust
  Abinger Common
  Surrey RH5 6TH
  01306–730871

GODINTON HOUSE (R. BLOMFIELD)
  Ashford
  Kent TN23 3BP
  01233–620773

GRAVETYE MANOR HOTEL (W. ROBINSON)
  Vowels Lane
  East Grinstead
  West Sussex RH19 4LJ
  01342–810567
  www.gravetyemanor.co.uk

GRAYTHWAITE HALL (T. MAWSON)
  Ulverston
  Cumbria LA12 8BA
  01539–531248

GREAT DIXTER
  Northiam
  East Sussex TN31 6PH
  01797–252878
  www.greatdixter.co.uk

HESTERCOMBE GARDENS
(LUTYENS AND JEKYLL)
  Cheddon Fitzpaine
  Taunton
  Somerset TA2 8LG
  01823–413923
  www.hestercombegardens.com

THE HILL (T. MAWSON)
  Corporation of London
  Inverforth Close
  London NW3 7EX
  0208–4555183

HILL HOUSE (C. R. MACKINTOSH)
  Upper Colquhoun Street
  Helensburgh
  Strathclyde G84 9AJ
  01436–673900
  www.nts.org.uk

HILL OF TARVIT (R. LORIMER)
  Cupar
  Fife KY15 5PB
  01334–653127
  www.nts.org.uk

KELLIE CASTLE (R. LORIMER)
  Pittenweem
  Fife KY10 2RF
  01333–720271
  www.nts.org.uk

KELMSCOTT MANOR (W. MORRIS)
The Society of Antiquaries
Lechlade
Gloucestershire GL7 3HJ
01367–252486
www.kelmscottmanor.co.uk

LEVENS HALL
Kendal
Cumbria LA8 0PD
01539–560321
www.levenshall.co.uk

LINDISFARNE CASTLE (LUTYENS AND JEKYLL)
Holy Island
Berwick-upon-Tweed
01289–389244
www.nationaltrust.org.uk

LITTLE ONN HALL (T. MAWSON)
Church Eaton
Stafford ST20 0UA
01785–840154
by appointment only

LLANGOED HALL (C. WILLIAMS-ELLIS)
Llyswen
Powys SLD3 OYP
01674–754525

LUGGERS HALL (A. PARSONS)
Springfield Lane
Broadway
Worcestershire WR12 7BT
01386–852040
www.luggershall.com

THE MANOR HOUSE (G. JEKYLL)
Upton Grey
Basingstoke
Hampshire RG25 2RD
www.gertrudejekyllgarden.co.uk

MOUNDSMERE MANOR (R. BLOMFIELD)
Preston Candover
Basingstoke
Hampshire RG25 2HE
01256–389207

MOUNT STEWART (G. JEKYLL)
Greyabbey
Newtonards
Co. Down BT22 2AD
www.nationaltrust.org.uk

MUNSTEAD WOOD (G. JEKYLL)
Godalming
Surrey GU7 1UN

OARE HOUSE (C. WILLIAMS-ELLIS)
Oare
Wiltshire SN8 4JQ
01672–562613

OWLPEN MANOR (N. JEWSON)
Uley
Gloucestershire GL11 5BZ
01453–86021
www.owlpen.com

PENSHURST PLACE
Tonbridge
Kent TN11 8DG
01892–870307
www.penshurstplace.com

PLAS BRONDANW (C. WILLIAMS-ELLIS)
Llanfrothen
Penrhyndeudraeth
Gwynedd LL48 6SW
01766–771136

PORTMEIRION (C. WILLIAMS-ELLIS)
Penrhyndeudraeth
Gwynedd LL48 6ET
01766–771331
www.portmeirion.com

THE PRIORY (P. HEALING)
Kemerton
Worcestershire
01386–725258
by appointment only

RED HOUSE (W. MORRIS)
Bexleyheath
Kent DA6 8JF
01494–755588
www.nationaltrust.org.uk

RIDLER GARDEN
7 St. Peter's Terrace
Swansea
Glamorgan SA2 0FW
01792–588217

RODMARTON MANOR (E. BARNSLEY)
Rodmarton
Gloucestershire GL7 6PF
01285–841253
www.rodmarton-manor.co.uk

SNOWSHILL MANOR (BAILLIE SCOTT)
Snowshill
Gloucestershire WR12 7JU
01386–852410
www.nationaltrust.org.uk

STANDEN (P. WEBB)
East Grinstead
West Sussex RH19 4NE
01342–323029
www.nationaltrust.org.uk

STOBHALL
By Perth
Perthshire PH2 6DR
www.gardensofscotland.org

TIRLEY GARTH (C. E. MALLOWS)
Tarporley
Cheshire
01829–732301
www.tirleygarth.com

WIGHTWICK MANOR
(A. PARSONS AND T. MAWSON)
Wolverhampton
West Midlands WV6 8EE
01902–761400
www.nationaltrust.org.uk

WYNDCLIFFE COURT (H. A. TIPPING)
St. Arvans
Monmouthshire NP16 6EY
01291–622352
by appointment only

YORK GATE
Adel
Leeds LS16 8DW
01132–678240
www.gardeners-grbs.org.uk

UNITED STATES

For further information, consult the Garden Conservancy's *Open Days Directory* (www.gardenconservancy.org), *National Geographic Guide to America's Public Gardens,* and James Massey and Shirley Maxwell's *Arts and Crafts Design in America: A State by State Guide* (Chronicle, 1998).

BEAUPORT
Sleeper-McCann House
75 Eastern Point Blvd.
Gloucester, Mass. 01930
(978) 283–0800
www.spnea.org

BLACKER HOUSE (GREENE & GREENE)
1177 Hillcrest Avenue
Pasadena, Calif. 91106
www.ugcs.caltech.edu~blacker

CORNISH COLONY GALLERY AND MUSEUM
Route 12A
Cornish, N.H. 01745
(603) 675–6000

CRAFTSMAN FARMS (G. STICKLEY)
2352 Route 10
Morris Plains, N.J.
(973) 540–1165
www.stickleymuseum.org

CRANBROOK ACADEMY (E. SAARINEN)
1221 North Woodward Avenue
Bloomfield Hills, Mich. 48303
(801) 645–3000
www.cranbrook.edu

DUMBARTON OAKS (B. FARRAND)
1703 32nd Street NW
Washington, D.C. 20007
(202) 339–6401
www.doaks.org

EL ALISAL (LUMMIS HOUSE)
200 East Avenue 43
Los Angeles, Calif. 90031
(213) 220–0546

FAIRSTED
Frederick Law Olmsted National
Historic Site
99 Warren Street
Brookline, Mass. 02146
(617) 566–3964
www.nps.gov

FRANK LLOYD WRIGHT HOME AND STUDIO
951 Chicago Avenue
Oak Park, Ill. 60302
(708) 848–1976
www.wrightplus.org

GAMBLE HOUSE (GREENE & GREENE)
4 Westmoreland Place
Pasadena, Calif. 91103
(818) 793–3334
www.gamblehouse.usc.edu

GERTRUDE JEKYLL GARDEN
AT THE GLEBE HOUSE
Hollow Road
Woodbury, Conn. 06798
(203) 263–2855
www.theglebehouse.org

GREEN ANIMALS TOPIARY GARDEN
380 Corys Lane
Portsmouth, R. I. 02871
(401) 683–1267
www.newportmansions.org

LADEW TOPIARY GARDENS
3535 Jarrettsville Pike
Monkton, Md. 21111
(301) 557–9570
www.ladewgardens.com

MADOO CONSERVANCY (R. DASH)
618 Main Street
Sagaponack, N.Y. 11962
(631) 537–8200
www.hamptons.com/madoo

RAGDALE FOUNDATION (H.V.D. SHAW)
1260 North Green Bay Road
Lake Forest, Il. 60045
(847) 234–1063
www.ragdale.org

ROBIE HOUSE (F. L. WRIGHT)
5757 South Woodlawn Avenue
Chicago, Il. 60637
(708) 848–1976
www.wrightplus.org

ROYCROFT CAMPUS AND INN (G. STICKLEY)
31 South Grove Street
East Aurora, N.Y. 14052
(716) 652–3333
www.roycroft.org

SAINT-GAUDENS NATIONAL HISTORIC SITE
Route 12A
Cornish, N.H. 03745
(603) 675–2175
www.sgnhs.org

SHELBURNE FARMS
Harbor Road
Shelburne, Vt. 05482
(802) 985–8686

STAN HYWET HALL AND GARDENS
(English Garden by E. B. Shipman)
714 North Portage Path
Akron, Ohio 44303
(330) 836–5533
www.stanhywet.org

TALIESIN (F. L. WRIGHT)
Highway 23
Spring Green, Wisc. 53588
(608) 588–7900
www.taliesinpreservation.org

WINTERTHUR MUSEUM AND GARDENS
(H. F. DU PONT)
Winterthur, Del. 19735
(302) 888–4600
www.winterthur.org

Index

Numbers in *italics* refer to illustrations.

Illustration Credits

Acknowledgments

This book could not have been written without benefit of the knowledge of numerous experts who, over the years, have enlightened me about Arts and Crafts architecture, decorative arts, and gardens. Among them are David Berman, the late John Brandon-Jones, John Burroughs, Rick Darke, Davyd Foard Hood, Margaret Richardson, Bruce Smith, David Streatfield, Robin Whalley, and Martin Wood. I would also like to thank all the homeowners and custodians who allowed me to tarry in their homes and gardens. These include William Benson, Mr. and Mrs. Simon Biddulph, Major and Mrs. John Birchall, Mr. and Mrs. John H. Bryan, Sir Robert and Lady Clark, Helen Dillon, Simon Dorrell and David Wheeler, Noel Gibbs, Sir Samuel Goldman, Nicholas and Karin Mander, Jean-Paul Marix-Evans, Mr. and Mrs. Hugh St. John-Mildmay, Mr. and Mrs. Charles Platt, the late Sibyl Spencer, and Rosamund Wallinger. In addition, William Brogden, Jane Brown, Rick Darke, Simon Dorrell, Robert Gordon and Marjorie Mann, Fenja Gunn, Ngaere Macray, Art Miller, Nan Blake Sinton, David Streatfield, Ann Uppington, Martin Wood, and many others generously showed me local private gardens. A special note of gratitude to Peter Herbert, whose hospitality leads me to imagine Gravetye Manor as my second home.

I would also like to thank the following individuals and organizations that have provided illustrations, information, or congenial venues for sharing my enthusiasm for the Arts and Crafts Movement with colleagues: Alice Pearson, curator, Blackwell; Bridgeman Art Library; J.R. Burrows and Company; Catha Grace Rambusch, Catalogue of Landscape Records, Wave Hill; the Cheltenham Museum; Christopher Wood Gallery; Camilla Costello, Country Life Picture Library; the Garden History Society; Mark Alan Hewitt; The Landscape Institute, Harvard University; Art Miller, archivist, Lake Forest College; the Lutyens Trust; the New England Garden History Society of the Massachusetts Horticultural Society; the Museum of Garden History; Susan Page Tillett, executive director, the Ragdale Foundation; the Rare and Manuscript Collections Cornell University Library; Jonathan Makepeace, assistant curator, Royal Institute of British Architects; the Royal Horticultural Society, Lindley Library; the Society of Architectural Historians; Lorna Condon, archivist, Society for the Preservation of New England Antiquities; the Surrey County Council; the Surrey Gardens Trust; David Berman, Trustworth Studios; Martin Durrant, V&A Images, and Linda Parry, deputy keeper, Victoria and Albert Museum; Dr. Lawrence Trevelyan Weaver; the William Morris Society.

Among the people who lent books or illustrations, I would like to thank Bonnie Briscoe, Fenja Gunn, Allyson Hayward, Marion Pressley, Nan Blake Sinton, Bruce Smith, Ann Uppington, Christopher Wood, and Martin Wood. I also owe a debt to the booksellers who found special editions, letters, or other treasured additions for my library: Robin Bledsoe, Anna Buxton, Jim Hinck and Ann Marie Wall, Daniel Lloyd, the late Timothy Mawson, Harvey Mendelsohn (who translated essential passages from Muthesius's *Das Englische Haus*), Jane Robie, David Wheeler (who found a near-complete run of *Country Life* magazine in a bookshop in Hay-on-Wye and allowed me to write about it in *Hortus*), the late Elisabeth Woodburn, and many others.

Thanks are also due to Ruth Peltason, former editor at Abrams, who initiated this project, to my editor, Elaine Stainton, to Robert McKee, who designed the book, and to Justine Keefe the production manager who saw it to completion. Especial thanks to Simon Dorrell, art editor of *Hortus*, who provided the pen-and-ink drawings of garden plans.

And last, but not least, a special acknowledgment to my husband, John R. Tankard, my intrepid house-and-garden-visiting companion, who frequently offered pithy comments about things I otherwise would have overlooked, bailed me out when my camera failed, and regularly procured items for our library, including a twenty-year run of *The Studio* magazine that he spotted moldering in a bookshop in Surrey.

Editor: Elaine M. Stainton
Designer: Robert McKee
Production Manager: Justine Keefe

Library of Congress Cataloging-in-Publication Data
Tankard, Judith B.
Gardens of the arts and crafts movement : reality and imagination / Judith B. Tankard.
    p. cm.
Includes bibliographical references (p.   ).
ISBN 0-8109-4965-2 (hardcover)
1. Arts and crafts gardens—England. 2. Arts and crafts gardens—United States.
3. Arts and crafts movement—England. I. Title.

SB454.3.A76T36 2004
712.6'0942—dc22

2004000877

Printed and bound in China

10 9 8 7 6 5 4 3 2 1

Harry N. Abrams, Inc.
100 Fifth Avenue
New York, N.Y. 10011
www.abramsbooks.com

Abrams is subsidiary of

LA MARTINIÈRE
GROUPE